BUDGETING BASICS

JACKSON E. RAMSEY
INEZ L. RAMSEY

BUDGETING
BASICS

HOW TO SURVIVE
THE BUDGETING PROCESS

A GROLIER COMPANY

FRANKLIN WATTS

New York   Toronto   1985

Library of Congress Cataloging in Publication Data

Ramsey, Jackson Eugene, 1938–
Budgeting basics.

Bibliography: p.
Includes index.
1. Budget in business.   I. Ramsey, Inez L.
II. Title.
HG4028.B8R35   1985   658.1'54   85-7109
ISBN 0-531-09580-0

July 86

CONTENTS

INTRODUCTION
TO BUDGETING

*"What is a budget and why
do we use budgets?"*

DEFINITION OF A BUDGET

Every organization, regardless of its type, should plan for its future activities. A budget is the translation of the future plans of the company into financial terms, i.e., dollars and cents. At the company level, the budget translates sales volume and production volume into dollar amounts, so that profit and the amount of cash the company will need to conduct its business in the future can be estimated. At the department level, the budget takes the level of work output expected and translates it into dollar estimates of future costs.

THE PLACE OF PROFITS
IN THE COMPANY

Profit is defined as the money the company receives for its goods and services (revenue) less the money needed to produce the goods and services (costs). Profits are the rewards to the company for manufacturing and marketing the products or services it produces. From these profits the company may (1) pay dividends to stockholders, (2) pay back money it has borrowed, or (3) reinvest the profits in new equipment or other items to help the company in the future. For most private companies, profit is the reason for existence of the organization. If there is inadequate profit, the owners of the company may become dissatisfied with management and may even remove the managers. If profits continue too low, the company may eventually be closed by its owners.

Non-profit organizations do not have profit as a goal of the organization. For conceptual accounting and budgeting purposes, however, non-profit organizations differ from profit-oriented organizations in only one major point: they do not pay dividends to stockholders. Organizations that consider themselves non-profit still need to generate an excess of revenue over costs to pay for loans for equipment purchased in the past, to purchase new equipment for the future, to expand services, or to hire additional personnel. In the non-profit sector, profit is often called "surplus," and loss is called "deficit." For our purposes in most of this book, the same principles apply to profit and non-profit organizations alike, although this is an oversimplification of a complicated subject. In Chapter 11, we will discuss some topics in non-profit budgeting.

FINANCIAL REPORTS

How are stockholders informed of the company's financial condition? Your company will publish an annual report for this purpose. In this report you will find three main financial reports: (1) the statement of changes in financial position, (2) the balance sheet, and (3) the statement of earnings.

The statement of changes in financial position reports on the cash flow of the company, including sources of funds and the purposes for which funds were used. This report deals with actual cash (money, checking accounts, and so on) and does not include money owed to the company or by the company or depreciation. It is a summary of a time period, say a year.

The balance sheet provides a snapshot of the firm's financial position at a given time period, say the end of a fiscal year. It includes statements of assets, liabilities, and shareholders' equity in the firm.

The statement of earnings provides a statement of revenue, costs, and profits of the company for a given time period, say a year. If you are not familiar with these financial statements, you may want to read Appendix A after finishing this chapter so that you will know how to read and understand them. You may want to obtain a copy of your company's annual report for your own information.

THE NEED FOR COST CONTROL

In theory, selling prices are determined by the marketing department and upper-level management. The prices must certainly include the cost of manufacture of the goods and services, but the manufacturing costs of one particular product may be only a portion of the input to the pricing decision. Supervisors and managers outside the sales department may have little or no control over the pricing and marketing decisions, hence they cannot directly affect the company's revenue.

Supervisors will, however, have a great deal of control over the costs and expenses of the departments they manage. In every job, the supervisor can make a strong attempt to get the work accomplished as cheaply as possible, given accepted quality levels and delivery schedules. Supervisors should attempt to control the actual costs that they can control as closely as possible. If every supervisor watches costs carefully, the net result will be lower total costs for the entire company.

An important part of every supervisor's job is to work within financial limits. Supervisors and managers should be proud of their ability to carry out the duties of their departments in as efficient a financial method as possible.

THE NEED TO PLAN FOR THE FUTURE

The goals and objectives of an organization are the basic starting points from which all of the organization's future plans should be derived, including the budget. Organizations should set goals in categories like profit, sales volume, production volume, and product or service quality. The organization may also set goals and objectives in less measurable areas like employee morale and community relations. The company's goals and objectives from which the budget is developed serve as a basis for future activities.

Why bother planning for the future? Perhaps the answer to this question is obvious, but it constantly amazes us how many organizations make no attempt to plan their goals and objectives, let alone their finances, for the future. Assuming the organization wishes to stay in existence in the future, it must translate its future plans into financial statements so that funds are available to carry out the company's activities.

The starting point of long-range planning is the products and services the company will offer customers in the future. Management must make decisions as to what current products and services to continue in the future, and what new products and services the company might want to add to their product lines. (A product line is a group of similar but carefully differentiated products, such as General Motors' product line of automobiles: Chevrolet, Pontiac, Oldsmobile, Buick, and Cadillac.) Once the decision on products is made, planning can begin on items like personnel needs, channels of product distribution, and factories and equipment.

All levels of managers must be thinking now of new products and services to offer customers in the future because the company will need to begin the planning to produce those products or services now. First- and second-level managers alone will not make the decisions on new products for the company for the future. You might, however, have excellent suggestions that should be passed along to the appropriate individuals. In any case, you may be asked for information about costs for new product components. You must recognize the importance of providing as accurate information as you can.

THE NEED FOR BUDGETS

Any company needs some idea of what monies it will earn in the future and what monies it will spend. The difference between revenue and costs is the profit the company will make. Budgets are also necessary to help with the detailed planning of sales and the detailed planning of costs.

Budgets are necessary for all the different departments of the company. The sales department must estimate the future volume of sales of each product or service to be sold as well as the price at which each item will be sold. The manufacturing departments must estimate the costs to produce each item or service to be produced. The finance department must estimate when the actual money will be coming in and when it will be spent so that there is enough money on hand to pay bills. All of these departments need to estimate future expenses as accurately as possible.

The budget also serves some non-financial purposes. In preparing a department budget, a sales budget, or the overall budget, the managers involved must look again at the assumptions on which their estimates of the future are based. The managers must reconsider their sales forecasts, production details, and cash flow predictions. They must make sure that the previous plans on which they based their budgets have not changed. In this sense, the budget also serves as a convenient document tying together different areas of the company.

We have assumed that our company under discussion is in business to make a profit. Today, however, many organizations are deliberately set up to be non-profit. For accounting and budgeting purposes in this book, there is no substantive difference between a profit-oriented company and a non-profit organization. A non-profit organization deliberately strives for a profit of zero. A budget is just as important for a non-profit organization as for one that is profit oriented. Planning the budget helps determine where costs should be incurred, and later analysis will help determine if the actual costs were in accordance with the original budget.

THE BUDGET CYCLE (BUDGETS AS A MANAGEMENT TOOL)

The budget is a financial plan of future profit, revenue, and costs. This future plan serves as the base for a cycle of management control activities. In this cycle, the first step is an estimate of future costs for a department for some time period, say a month. When the month arrives, actual costs for the month are recorded by the accounting system and charged to the department. A variance report is issued comparing the budgeted and actual costs. If the actual costs of individual items differ (vary) from the budgeted costs, the department supervisor can be asked to investigate and report on these cost variances. Based upon this variance analysis, future budgets may need to be modified, or production methods may need to be changed to bring the actual costs in line with the budget. (Further discussion of managerial cost control is provided in Chapter 7.)

As a means of estimating profits and revenues, and as a basis for cost control, the budget is very useful. It also is useful to management for other planning purposes. Based upon a review of past budget records, management may determine that a product or service is not worth retaining because of lack of profit or volume of service. Past budget records also help management determine if new products should be added to a product line. Again, once future products are determined, information is available to management for decisions on new-equipment purchases, for potential changes in number of employees, and for potential bank loans or other borrowing.

THE SUPERVISOR'S AND MANAGER'S RESPONSIBILITY FOR BUDGETING

For a budget to serve as a useful document and not another piece of paper to be ignored, it must originate (or at least have substantial input) from the supervisor or manager who must carry out the budget. That is, if the budget is developed by upper-level managers without any input from supervisors, the supervisor may not feel the obligation to carry out the budget nearly as much as if the supervisor had a say in preparing the budget.

For operating cost budgets in particular, the supervisor is the management-level representative closest to where the work is actually accomplished. The supervisor is then best qualified to make the most accurate judgments on what the honest estimates of costs for the future will be. The supervisor must be kept informed by upper-level management of possible future changes in items like production levels and new-equipment purchases, so that the budget estimates reflect the most accurate data. This does not mean that budgeting responsibility rests only with the supervisor. Upper-level management has overall control of the budgeting function, like all other activities, and may insist that past cost performance be matched or improved.

Nevertheless, the supervisor is the individual with day-to-day control of many of the costs of the operating budget. The supervisor must be committed to the budget as a practical tool, or there is little chance the budget will actually be met.

TYPES OF BUDGETS

*"What are the different types of budgets
and why do we need them?"*

Budgets are prepared for a number of different purposes. Even though you as a supervisor or manager may not use all of them, it will help you with the budgets you do use if you understand the different types of budgets. Since a budget is a plan, however, let us first look at the overall planning process and its role in developing different types of budgets.

PLANNING

Just as individuals need to plan in order to achieve long- and short-term goals, companies of all sizes need a formal, effective planning system if the necessary profits are to be realized for successful competition in the marketplace. As you plan for a special vacation, you may consult maps to plan the most effective route, compare costs for traveling via automobile or other forms of transportation, set up an itinerary of places to be visited, develop timelines, and estimate costs to be incurred. Without such planning your vacation may degenerate into disaster. Many companies have failed in the long run due to lack of such foresight in business planning.

Operating managers at all levels need to know how to plan in order to operate their departments successfully. Managers cannot plan effectively unless they themselves understand the company's long- and short-term goals and objectives and have had opportunity to give input to those plans. Managers at all levels of the organization should be aware of the company's goals and objectives so that decisions they make are consistent within the organization's overall plans. How then does a company plan for its future?

Long-Range Planning (Strategic Planning)

In long-range planning (say five years or more), upper-level management will address questions related to topics such as products, markets, capital investments, research, employee relations, profits, and return on investments. In order to plan effectively for the future, these managers will also need to have a clear overall picture of the company's present strengths and weaknesses in areas such as productivity, products, markets, profits, return on investment, capital holdings, and other factors related to the company's economic health.

Long-range planning is, of course, complex due to the uncertainties of the future, with the longer the planning period the greater the uncertainty. For this reason, long-range plans must be periodically reviewed and adjusted by management. Management will have to take many factors into consideration in planning for the future, including:

1. Technology developments

2. Marketing forecasts

3. Economic factors, such as interest rates, rate of inflation, raw materials' costs, and labor supplies

4. Political factors, such as possible new legislation affecting the company.

Financial officials of the company will need to collect, analyze, and report information to be used in forecasting the future. Internal sources of data include historical data and reports by company sales executives in the field. Financial analysts may calculate sophisticated forecasting mathematical models and other statistics such as break-even analysis and return-on-investment calculations to provide data for the decision-making process.

Larger companies may develop financial reports (strategic budgets) such as:

1. Profit plans for projected income

2. A cash plan for expected receipts and payments

3. A procurement budget for anticipated expenses for materials, supplies, and other services

4. A statement of proposed assets and owners' equities (see Balance Sheet, Appendix A).

From this process, upper-level management should develop a statement of the broad goals, for the long run of the firm, to be communicated to all levels of management. These goals should speak to questions such as:

1. Expected size and scope of operations

2. Attitudes toward customers

3. Employee relations

4. Services or products to be offered

5. Anticipated product diversification

6. Product quality

7. Capital-investment plans

8. Commitment toward research.

Goals statements would answer questions like:

1. What products will the firm continue to make in the future?

2. What products are we considering adding to our product line?

3. Which of our current customers do we anticipate selling to in the future?

4. What new groups do we anticipate as future customers?

5. What changes in society do we anticipate that will affect our business?

In this manner management can provide a framework within which operating managers can themselves make informed and intelligent decisions when developing budgets.

As you can see, long-range planning is a very complex task and a very time-consuming one. As a line supervisor or manager, you will have no direct responsibility at this level of decision making. You may have ideas, however, which deserve to be considered by management in the planning process. Be willing to make suggestions which could help to improve the company's financial position. Present your proposal in a formal, well-documented manner with reasonable cost figures. Frame your proposal in terms of your idea's place within the company's goals and objectives.

Also, in developing long-term goals, management may ask you to supply cost figures for a proposed production change or ask your advice on problems involved in proposed new scheduling or machine utilization. You should supply the most complete and accurate information you can to the decision makers. Make an effort to be as informed as possible of your company's long-term goals. Ask your supervisor for any information you may need. In addition, you should appreciate the fact that long-range planning is indeed a complex problem and that your department is not the only department which has to be considered in the budgeting process. Budgeting decisions coming to you from your supervisor may be reflecting some long-range plan about which you have not been told.

If no formal communications line has been established between management levels, you may have to second-guess your company's goals from what upper-level managers do or do not do. In today's competitive marketplace, however, even small and medium-sized firms are becoming more sophisticated in their long-range planning and managerial information systems.

Short-Term Planning

Management will need to translate long-range goals into more specific short-term objectives. These objectives are specific in nature and can be quantified. Specific objectives may be developed for a specific planning cycle, say three years. These objectives are then translated into a three-year operating plan with performance objectives to be met for each year of the three-year period. As an operating manager, you will be working with short-term (annual) objectives. These short-term objectives will be developed for all areas within the company.

Let us say that the company's objective is to increase profits 10 percent per year for the next three years. The objective this year is to increase profit before taxes by 10 percent. This company objective will be translated into specific performance objectives for the sales department, the manufacturing department, the finance department, and other departments within the company. Your part in contributing to this objective may translate into increased production of certain products by some definite amount and into production of those products at some specified cost per unit. These short-term performance objectives translate into: (1) levels of production, (2) amounts of inventory to be carried, (3) labor, materials, and other services required, and (4) other short-term decisions. In other words, these performance objectives serve as the starting point for your budget. Your beginning budget will reflect what you feel is necessary in terms of labor, materials, and other costs to meet your assigned performance objectives. Once your budget is approved by upper-level management, it reflects how much you have been authorized to spend to fulfill those objectives. As an operating manager, you may be evaluated on your ability to meet your assigned performance objectives.

Planning Cycle

Goals.   In any form of planning the first step is to develop a general list of goals to be achieved. These goals may be more philosophic in nature, rather than a specific plan of action. For example, management may have defined a goal of expansion of geographical outlets for product sales. That is, one of our long-term goals is the geographic expansion of sales territory.

Objectives.   From our goal statement, we need to define specific performance objectives which can be quantified and measured. We do this so that it is clear to managers at all levels what we plan to accomplish. We can also establish specific performance objectives against which progress will be measured. Our objective might be translated into targets for the planning year, 198X–198X + 1. These targets might include:

1. The sales department will increase the number of sales outlets handling our products in the state of North Carolina by 10 percent.

is defined as equipment that will be used for a number of years in the future, earning profits for the company in the future as well as in the present year. Capital equipment can vary from a new building to an expensive machine tool in the factory to a laboratory testing device to a word processor for a secretary.

Capital budgeting deals specifically with estimating the costs of the new pieces of equipment and the savings, if any, to be generated from the new pieces of equipment. Capital budgeting is assuming greater importance in the 1980s in the United States because of the increased emphasis on productivity and the use of capital equipment as a major method to improve productivity. In addition, many suggestions for the future of the United States economy revolve around high-technology companies with even greater concentrations of capital equipment per employee.

Capital budgeting deals not only with the costs and savings of a new piece of equipment but also with the ways in which supervisors and managers can justify to upper-level management the purchase of the piece of equipment from its savings. As a supervisor, you should be concerned about the quantity and quality of equipment in the areas you supervise. An understanding of how you can support requests for new equipment to upper-level management is very important. We will discuss capital budgeting in detail in Chapter 9.

PRODUCTION OPERATING BUDGETS

The budget that deals with the costs for the goods and services produced, either on a department basis or on a product basis, is called an operating budget.

You as a supervisor may be told to control the costs in your department as closely as possible and not to worry about (1) the prices charged for the goods and services you produce and (2) the costs outside your department. That is, you may be told to concentrate on the costs you can influence (control) and let others worry about other costs and revenue. The concept of an operating budget is to accumulate and report the costs at the supervisor level, the level of management closest to the employees. Most of the balance of this book will deal with the details of operating budgets.

NON-PRODUCTION OPERATING BUDGETS

While we have talked of budgeting primarily in terms of you as a supervisor budgeting for your production department, other non-production departments such as sales, purchasing, and stores, will also have budgets.

For example, the sales department will have its own internal operating budget covering items like salaries, advertising, and travel expenses. It will also have a budget for sales by product and by product line, and probably even a budget by sales to largest customers.

Purchasing will have a budget that will estimate all of their purchases for the next year. It may also estimate the dollar amounts that will be spent for major purchased cost items and may even estimate dollar amounts to be spent with major vendors. Purchasing will also have its own internal operating budget that will consist of items like salaries, travel, stationery, and supplies.

Most companies will have a separate stores department to manage inventory. In some cases, however, the stores function may be combined in a shipping and receiving department. In a few cases, inventory control will be split among the purchasing and manufacturing departments.

The stores department will have its own internal operating budget with items like salaries, supplies, and repairs. The stores department will also have a budget for the dollar amount of materials in inventory at any one time. This should be broken down into categories of finished-goods inventory, work-in-process inventory (inventory actually being worked on in the manufacturing departments or stored in an uncompleted state), and raw-materials inventory. In many organizations, finished-goods inventory is controlled by the sales department and work-in-process and raw-materials inventory by the manufacturing department. All of these inventories should be expressed in dollar amounts and may be broken down into categories of products or specific materials. While the stores department may have to control the inventory, the total dollar amount, particularly in finished-goods and raw-materials inventories, may be set by upper-level management.

As a department supervisor, you may not need to worry about inventory control. It may affect you, however, if pressures to reduce work in process inventory cause uneven work flow within your department. Likewise, pressures to reduce raw-materials inventory could mean that raw materials are not available when you need them, and their absence could disrupt the work flow in your department. If you feel that decisions are being made about inventory levels that could have a negative effect on your department, make sure you mention your concern to the appropriate managers.

FIXED AND FLEXIBLE BUDGETING

The starting point for most operating budgets is a volume of output to be produced by your department. You then calculate your operating budget based upon that volume of output. During the time period you are working, say a month, the actual output you produce may change. In most accounting systems the accounting department will accumulate actual costs during the month (accrue) and, at the end of the month, issue a report comparing the actual costs to the budgeted costs. You may then be asked to analyze and explain the differences. (Details of this budget cycle will be discussed in more depth in Chapter 8.) If you compare the actual costs to the planned-production budget, you are treating the planned production as a "fixed" budget. If you adjust the budget costs to reflect the actual units of output, then you are comparing actual costs to budgeted costs for the same number of units of output. This is called a "flexible" budget.

For example, suppose output for your department for July was estimated to be 9,000 units and you based all your budgeted cost estimates on that figure. During July, however, you actually produced 10,000 units. A fixed budget would compare your actual expenses for 10,000 units to the budgeted expenses for 9,000 units. A flexible budget would readjust your original budget to include costs for 10,000 units and then compare the actual cost of 10,000 units to the readjusted budgeted cost of 10,000 units.

Most of the time a fixed cost system is used. Why? When you are using a monthly budget, the differences in planned and actual production are seldom large enough to be worth the trouble of revision, i.e., the time and the cost involved in reworking the budget. Changing the cost estimates once you have decided upon a volume of output may require disproportionate work because of the different types of costs, i.e., fixed, variable, or semi-variable, involved. (These types of costs will be discussed later.) Flexible budgets are becoming more common today, however, since the use of computerized spreadsheets has greatly simplified the revision process.

FUNDS FLOW AND CASH FLOW

Finally, in order to understand the planning/budgeting process, you should be familiar with the concepts of funds flow and cash flow as distinct from the more familiar concept of profit and loss. An individual in the finance or accounting department will be responsible for developing funds and cash flow. Although funds flow and cash flow are more important at the corporate level, you should understand the effect of these corporate activities in the decision-making process.

Funds Flow

"Funds" is the term used to describe the circulating capital in a firm. In most cases, funds enter the firm in the form of cash and credit. They are converted into manufactured goods and then reconverted into cash and credit through the sale of these manufactured goods.

Generally, the first cash into a firm is provided by the original stockholders. Once the company is established, credit is obtained from suppliers. Additional cash may be obtained from bank loans, sales of stock, and retained earnings. Needed equipment may be leased. In a manufacturing firm, cash and credit are applied to the purchase of raw materials, labor, supplies, energy, and so on. Through manufacturing, these raw materials are converted into work in process and then into finished-goods inventory. With the sale of finished products on credit, the finished goods are converted into accounts receivable. Collection of accounts receivable reinstates the cash to start a new cycle. Normally, the value of the company will be higher at the end of this cycle than at the beginning. This increase in value is the profit the company earned by the manufacturing process. (If there is a decrease in value at the end of the cycle, the company has suffered a loss.)

The cash position of the company may be higher or lower at the end of a period than at the beginning, regardless of the profit. The company's cash balance will rise if the cash receipts of the period exceed the cash disbursements.

If the reverse is true, the cash balance will fall. On the other hand, profit and loss depend on whether sales (both cash and *credit*) plus other revenues for the period exceed the costs of operation.

In general, the sources and uses of funds must balance out over the fiscal year. If funds inflow exceeds funds outflow, the corporate treasurer may invest the difference in short-term assets, like marketable securities. If funds outflow exceeds funds inflow, the corporate treasurer must make up the difference with short-term borrowing.

In general, the sources of funds include:

1. Net income before dividends
2. Depreciation
3. Reduction in cash
4. Sale of marketable securities
5. Increase in long-term debt
6. Increase in short-term debt
7. Increase in other liabilities
8. Sale of stock.

The uses of funds include:

1. Increases in inventory
2. Increases in receivables
3. Increase in cash
4. Purchase of marketable securities
5. Decrease in debt
6. Decrease in accounts payable

7. Capital investment

8. Dividends.

Cash Flow

Cash flow deals with the actual flow of money (dollars, coins, checks, and so on) in and out of the firm. Even if the company is making a reasonable profit, it can still be forced to go out of business if it cannot pay its current bills. A growing, profitable company is likely to require additional cash for investment in receivables, inventories, and fixed assets.

Two major items make up most of the difference between funds flow and cash flow: (1) credit and (2) depreciation. The extension of credit to customers and the use of credit from suppliers (including the government in the case of deferred taxes) means that the cash may not flow in and out as the sales and expenses are incurred (accrued).

In addition, depreciation is an expense of doing business and is charged as such against revenue. Depreciation lowers profits and taxes, but, in fact, depreciation is not paid out to anyone as cash. Depreciation costs are cash which may be retained by the company for other purposes.

In the newspapers you read of companies that have a loss year after year but still stay in business. This is often because depreciation causes them to report an accounting loss, but in fact their cash flow is still positive.

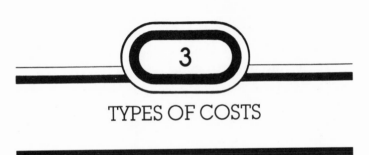

3

TYPES OF COSTS

*"What are the different types of costs
and how do they behave?"*

Costs are the dollars and cents spent to produce the goods
and services of your company. Costs include every dollar
spent by the company, regardless of what the money is spent
for. Knowing the total amount the company spends in a
year is important, of course. It is, however, of little use to
the manager or supervisor who must deal with costs on a
daily, not yearly, basis. There are many different types of
costs, however, and many different ways in which they can
behave. There are also many different ways in which the
costs can be expressed and broken down for more practical
use. This chapter will introduce most of these ways.

FIXED, VARIABLE,
AND SEMI-VARIABLE COSTS

One method of breaking down all costs is into categories
of fixed costs, variable costs, and semi-variable costs.

1. Fixed costs are costs that remain constant over a given time period throughout the normal expected production range. Examples include items like managers' salaries, rent, secretarial salaries, and depreciation of capital equipment.

2. Variable costs are those costs that increase or decrease in direct proportion to output. An example is most materials used in actually producing the products you sell (direct materials). That is, if output increases 10 percent, the amount of money spent for direct materials increases 10 percent. Another example, for most organizations, is the wages paid to individuals who directly produce your output (direct labor). Again, if output increases 10 percent, the direct labor should increase 10 percent.

3. Semi-variable costs are costs that vary with output, increasing and decreasing as output increases and decreases, but not in direct proportion to output. For example, if output increases 10 percent, machine repair might go up 20 percent due to the heavier usage. (Or machine repair could go up only 3 percent, if the previous usage was light.) Clerical costs and quality-control costs are other examples of semi-variable costs. Leased warehousing is also a semi-variable cost, but one that varies in a step fashion. You pay the lease at a flat rate until the warehouse is full, then you must lease more facilities.

It is important to understand that although fixed costs remain fixed in total per time period, such costs vary per unit of output. That is, the same fixed costs must be spread over the units of output produced, regardless of how many are produced. For example, if your department fixed costs are $10,000 per month, and your output is 4,000 units, your average fixed cost per unit is $2.50 that month. If, on the other hand, you can increase production to 5,000 units per month, your average fixed cost per unit drops to $2. Thus, fixed costs present an opportunity for decreasing average unit costs by greater output per time period. In a continuous process plant (like a paper mill, sewage treatment plant, or oil refinery), for example, if equipment is down and production is lost, the same fixed costs must be spread over fewer units of output, and average unit costs will be higher.

Unliked fixed costs, variable costs vary in total per time period but remain constant per unit of output. If you produced 4,000 units at a variable cost of $8 per unit, the total cost would be $32,000. If you can increase production to 5,000 units, your variable cost per unit would remain at $8, but your total variable costs would increase to $40,000. Thus, to decrease variable cost per unit you must decrease the labor and/or material content. Increasing output by itself will not lower variable cost per unit.

Semi-variable costs exhibit the characteristics of both fixed and variable costs. Some portions of the semi-variable costs will increase with increases in output, while other portions will not. While estimation of semi-variable costs for future production is not as easy as that of fixed and variable costs, specific methods to help you estimate them are discussed in Chapters 6, 7, and 8.

All of these types of costs are important, but the way to control and minimize costs will vary depending upon the degree to which the total costs are made up of fixed, variable, and semi-variable components. In general, a department budget will include items made up of each of these three types of costs.

Exhibit 3–1 shows a graphic example of these three types of costs and shows a total cost element composed of all three types. Exhibit 3–1 plots costs on the vertical axis and quantity of output on the horizontal axis. The costs are

EXHIBIT 3-1

Fixed, Variable, and Semi-Variable Costs

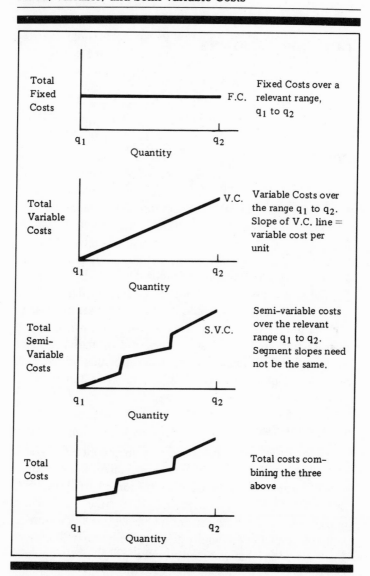

shown over a reasonable production range, from output quantity q_1 to output quantity q_2.

COST BREAKDOWNS

As an additional approach, costs can be broken down into the broad categories of direct labor, indirect labor, direct materials, and indirect materials. In the budget forms we will develop in the next chapter, we will break these categories down into more detailed sub-categories. Nevertheless, it is useful to introduce these four categories at this stage. Every cost in the company can be assigned to one of these categories.

Direct Labor

Direct labor is defined as the labor that is directly used in producing the goods or services you produce. That is, in a factory environment it would be the machinist, the assembler, or the finisher who works directly on the products you manufacture. In a retail store, it would be the floor sales personnel. Direct labor is often called by other terms, such as factory labor or hourly labor.

Indirect Labor

Indirect labor is all labor necessary to produce the goods and services manufactured, excluding direct labor. Examples of indirect labor include supervision and management, secretarial support, janitorial service, and the maintenance department. That is, these individuals support the direct-labor personnel who actually produce the goods and services and thus contribute indirectly to the production of goods and services. In most budgeting systems, indirect labor may be broken down into a number of sub-categories such as salaried labor, repair labor, and office labor.

Direct Materials

Direct materials are defined as those materials which become a part of the goods or services you are producing. In most budgeting systems, direct materials are broken into sub-categories, such as steel, plastic, wood, and purchased components. Direct materials may sometimes also be called production materials or just plain "materials."

Indirect Materials

Indirect materials are all materials used by the company which are not direct materials. Examples in production include lubricants, tooling, cleaning supplies, and processing supplies. For non-production activities, indirect materials could include items like secretarial supplies, computer paper, and cleaning supplies. In actual budget forms, indirect materials are normally broken down into a number of sub-categories, such as process supplies, lubricants, and cleaning supplies.

OVERHEAD COSTS

"Overhead cost," is a term widely used but seldom precisely defined. The implication is a indirect cost outside your control that is charged to your department or unit. Definition of "overhead costs" varies from company to company. If you are a department supervisor, you may have charged back to your department budget a portion of the cost of salaries of upper-level management. That is, these indirect labor costs might show up on your department budget as an overhead cost. Likewise, depreciation of capital equipment is an indirect cost that may be treated as overhead on your departmental budget. If you work in a plant or location with headquarters elsewhere, a portion of the corporate headquarters expenses might be allocated back to your plant. These would also be considered overhead costs.

Remember again the term "overhead costs" is imprecise. It identifies a concept of costs not under your control applied to your unit. We will instead use the term "indirect costs" in this book because of the lack of a clear-cut definition of "overhead costs." If the latter term is used by your company, make sure you have a clear understanding of what costs make up overhead costs.

COST ALLOCATION

Cost allocation involves dividing up a cost among a number of departments or cost centers. For example, a manager may supervise seven departments. In figuring the total cost of operation of each of those departments, the manager's salary must be divided up among those departments. There are a number of ways in which the manager's salary might be divided. It might be divided equally among the seven departments. It might be divided among the departments in proportion to the amount of time the manager actually spent working with each department. (This might vary from week to week or month to month.) It could also be divided in proportion to the number of people in each department, to the volume of work in each department, or to the dollar value of work in each department. The way in which the manager's salary is divided is called the basis for the allocation. In general, the costs to be allocated fall into the indirect labor and indirect materials categories.

In Chapter 5, we will discuss the practical methods of cost allocation.

COST MEASUREMENT

A budget is an estimate of future costs. Many times, however, the basis for a budget is the past cost structure. As noted earlier, in the budget cycle you compare budgeted costs for an item with the actual costs recorded for the budgeted time period. Thus, it is appropriate to introduce here the sources of data for the actual costs.

The dollar amounts that you use for your budgets come from a number of different sources. All labor hours and/or costs are recorded on some internal documents.

For a direct labor employee, this could be a time card where an individual clocks in and out on specific jobs. For the engineering department, individuals could fill out daily or weekly job sheets where they allocate their time to specific account numbers. For an upper-level manager or secretary, all of their time may be routinely charged to one account number. These cost-control records are generally also used for payroll purposes. Thus, labor costs are fairly well documented.

Almost every company has a purchase order form to order purchased materials. Purchased items will have a cost listed on this purchase order, even if it is only an estimate. This cost along with any shipping and receiving charges can be charged directly to the department or unit placing the order, or can be charged to an inventory account.

To take materials or supplies from a storage area generally requires some internal material requisition. This internal requisition lists the department or unit requesting the materials so that the accounting department can then charge back the materials to the correct user.

Non-cash items like depreciation are assigned directly by the accounting department from their internal paperwork.

In general, even the smallest company has some fairly clear-cut system of making sure that all costs can be easily measured and that they can be easily transferred to the appropriate department or unit.

CONTROLLABLE COSTS

Controllable costs are costs that can be directly controlled at a given level of management. Put another way, controllable costs are those that can be directly influenced by a supervisor or manager within a given time period. In theory, all costs are controllable at some level of management. The supervisor may have some control over overtime costs and scrap costs but will have no control over depreciation or employee benefits. Employee benefits, however, may be controllable (at least to some degree) by the industrial-relations manager or the factory manager. Corporate overhead costs may not be controllable by the factory manager but are controllable by corporate management. The budget reports that we will be discussing in detail will include both costs that you as a supervisor can control and costs that you cannot control. Obviously, controllable costs should receive more of your attention than uncontrollable costs.

Caution! People often assume that variable and semi-variable costs are controllable and that fixed costs are not. This is not true! There are different ways to control fixed costs and variable costs, but both types of costs are made up of many controllable elements.

SEASONAL COSTS

Seasonal costs are costs that vary with the seasons of the year. Heat, for example, might be necessary only in the winter. Higher electricity costs for air conditioning will be normal in the summer. Replacement personnel for individuals on vacation might also be heavier during the summer months. In addition, production operations might require additional costs depending upon the season of the year. Additional steam may be necessary in winter months to keep pipes from freezing. Special cooling of water in summer months might be necessary to maintain a correct temperature level.

Seasonal costs do not show up as such in any budgeting or reporting system. They are semi-variable costs that you must include in your budgeting. What is important is that you recognize that these costs may vary with the season of the year and make sure that they are properly estimated in your budget.

UNIT TOTAL COSTS

In our work with budgets you will be introduced to several manufacturing cost statistics, such as unit cost. Unit cost is simply an average cost. We determine unit cost by dividing some specified cost factor by the total number or volume of units produced. We talked about unit costs in our discussion of fixed costs earlier in this chapter. For example, if you produced 4,000 units of output at a total cost of $48,000, the average total unit cost would be $12 per unit of output, calculated by dividing $48,000 by 4,000 units.

Note that this average total unit cost is correct only for one level of output. Since the $48,000 cost figure is made up of fixed, semi-variable, and variable cost components, a change in production output means the average cost will not vary in proportion. That is, the total costs to produce 3,000 units of output might be $39,000 or $13 per unit.

Unit costs can be used for many purposes within the firm. As an operations manager, you may be supplied with unit-cost figures by your accounting department for each month and for each job as a measurement of work produced. Using unit costs, you may compare the unit cost for each month's production or for each job's production as a means of comparing work performance each month. Thus, unit costs can be used as one method for determining cost variability. If you find significant variability in your unit-cost figures, you should attempt to determine the reasons for the variability in performance, as a cost-control measure.

Measurement of costs is important for providing data for the internal decision-making process as well. Your sales department, for example, will use unit-cost figures as one input for determining the unit price at which the product will be sold. Upper-level management may also use unit-cost figures in determining total product-line profitability and as a cost-control measure.

COST CENTERS, PROFIT CENTERS, AND REVENUE CENTERS

"How do we gather profits, revenues, and costs and report them in forms useful to management?"

A major objective of every company is to make a profit, or at least to break even. The basic formula that controls all operations of the firm is $Pr = R - C$ (profit equals revenue minus costs). It is thus logical to gather costs in terms of these three components: profit, revenue, and costs.

PROFIT CENTER

A profit center is an organizational unit, activity, or product where all of the elements of revenue and costs can be accumulated to calculate the profit. The entire company is, of course, a profit center. For a large company, more detailed profit centers could be a specific manufacturing plant, if sales can be allocated to that plant, or a specific division. Costs could also be allocated to different products so that we could accumulate revenues and costs and calculate an expected profit for each product in a product line.

A profit center concept application is of limited use for most supervisors or managers because they do not have control over all of the elements of cost and revenue. While the amount of profits of the company is important to all employees, it is of more significance to upper-level managers since they may have the ability to influence most revenue and cost components. In addition, it is upper-level management, not individual supervisors, that will be responsible to the owners for company profit.

AN EXAMPLE FOR THIS BOOK—
THE HARRISONBURG
OFFICE EQUIPMENT
MANUFACTURING COMPANY

To make the details of accounting, finance, and budgeting more meaningful, detailed examples are necessary. To aid in the explanation of these details, we have created a mythical company and will provide examples for this company throughout this book. We hope that the use of a consistent set of examples will simplify understanding of these concepts and will aid in tying together all the topics in this book.

The Harrisonburg Office Equipment Manufacturing Company is a marketing and manufacturing company having sales of about $6 million a year. It produces a line of office furniture, such as desks, tables, chairs, file cabinets, waste baskets, and partition paneling. Most of the furniture is sold to retail stores for their resale, although some large customers are handled by a sales force at the factory. Most sales are within a 300-mile range of the company's headquarters and factory.

The company has only one factory, and at this same

location has its accounting and marketing operations. The company employs about 500 people, 350 hourly employees in the factory and 150 salaried employees in the office and factory. The products are manufactured from sheet metal, wood, and wood veneer. Some components are purchased. The factory operations involve receiving the raw materials, cutting and bending them to size and shape, machining and finishing the components, assembling them into finished units, and shipping the finished units.

Other details of our mythical Harrisonburg Office Equipment Manufacturing Company will be introduced in later chapters.

PROFIT-CENTER BUDGET FORMAT

Every company should budget an expected profit forecast for the future. Most firms will do this on a monthly, quarterly, and yearly basis. Some firms will even make five- and ten-year profit forecasts.

The format used for the profit-center budget format is usually the same as the profit-and-loss form for the company. These forms will vary greatly from one company to another.

An example of a profit-center budget form is shown in Exhibit 4-1. The form illustrated includes the major categories of revenue and costs that are found in most company reports. It is the profit forecast for an entire company—our mythical Harrisonburg Office Equipment Manufacturing Company—for the month of October. It lists reasonable dollar figures for each line item to round out the concept, although what is important at this stage is the revenue and cost categories, not the actual dollar amounts.

Revenues.   Anticipated sales for all products for October are listed. This is a net dollar amount, with an allowance for returned items and bad debts subtracted. Other

EXHIBIT 4-1

Profit-Center Budget Form

HARRISONBURG OFFICE EQUIPMENT
MANUFACTURING COMPANY
PROFIT-CENTER BUDGET-COMPANY
OCTOBER, 198X

Sales	$492,611
Other Revenue	3,161
Total Revenue	495,772
Cost of Goods Sold	240,017
Selling and Administrative Costs	81,517
Depreciation	65,371
Interest Expense	9,432
Total Costs	396,337
Profit Before Taxes	99,435
Net Taxes	40,174
Profit After Taxes	$59,261

revenue includes items like royalties, collection of bad debts, dividends from investments, and interest income. Together, these add to $495,772 in total revenue.

Costs.   Cost of goods sold includes all the manufacturing costs to produce the goods and services sold. It includes direct materials, direct labor, and indirect labor and materials that are used in the manufacturing process. Thus factory supervision and management costs are included in cost of goods sold. Selling and administrative costs are the costs for the non-manufacturing activities like marketing, accounting, and personnel. Selling and administrative costs are indirect labor and indirect material costs. Depreciation is the cost category where capital equipment the firm has purchased is written off as a monthly expense. That is, depreciation is the legal method of transferring the capital equipment from the asset accounts on the balance sheet to the profit-and-loss form to reflect the using up of the asset. (Depreciation will be discussed in detail in later chapters, and the balance sheet concept is discussed in Appendix A.) Interest expense is the interest charged in October for money the company has borrowed from banks and other lending institutions. Adding these costs components gives a total estimated monthly cost for October of $396,337.

Profits.   Subtracting total costs from total revenue gives an expected profit before taxes of $99,435. Subtracting estimated net taxes of $40,174 gives a "bottom line" profit-after-taxes estimate of $59,261.

REVENUE CENTER

A revenue center measures amount of sales of that organizational unit or product. The company itself is a revenue center for all of its sales. A revenue center could also be the sales for a division for a large company. For a chain of retail stores, a revenue center could be the revenue generated by one store. Revenue centers are of most use in sales departments since the goals and objectives of the managers in the sales department are normally set in terms of dollars or units of sales. While revenue centers may be of little day-to-day use for non-marketing supervisors and managers, they are important to the overall company.

REVENUE-CENTER BUDGET FORMAT

The actual budget forms used by individual companies for their revenue centers will vary greatly from company to company. Exhibit 4–2 shows an example revenue-center form for the Harrisonburg Office Equipment Manufacturing Company.

Exhibit 4–2 shows the revenue for the entire company for October. Estimated sales in dollars are listed for the company's main product lines: desks, tables, chairs, and partitions. At the company level, items that are sold in small dollar volume, such as wastebaskets, are grouped as Other. Within each major category, sales are estimated by major product, such as desk model D–7, or by model line, such as similar types of chairs grouped as model line C–5. These sales estimates have had subtracted an allowance for customer returns and bad debts. Thus, the total estimate of revenue for the company for October is $492,611.

Exhibit 4–2 is actually the summary revenue for the whole company. You would start with a revenue form for each individual product, estimate the sales of each product separately, and then combine the individual estimates into a company estimate.

COST CENTER

For most supervisors or managers outside the sales department, the concept of gathering costs by a work group, department, or any such easily grouped activity is by far the most useful (and most common) budgeting technique. If you are in charge of a group of twenty people carrying out work, you can influence the costs of that group but probably not the sales quantity or price of the product you are working

EXHIBIT 4–2

Revenue-Center Budget Form

HARRISONBURG OFFICE EQUIPMENT
MANUFACTURING COMPANY
REVENUE-CENTER BUDGET-COMPANY
OCTOBER, 198X

NET SALES

Desk: Model D–4	$71,371	
D–7	31,019	
D–8	81,734	
D–11	30,711	
Total Desks		214,835
Tables: Model T–6	41,322	
T–7	27,518	
T–8	18,542	
T–9	7,428	
Total Tables		94,810
Chairs: Model Line C–4	71,512	
C–5	28,473	
C–7	7,411	
Total Chairs		107,396
Partitions: Model Line P–1	40,717	
P–2	15,468	
P–4	5,432	
Total Partitions		61,617
Other		13,953
Total Net Sales		$492,611

on. There is thus no logical reason to attempt to attribute revenue of the firm directly to your work group. (This can be done on a theoretical basis; it is not normally worth the trouble and effort involved.)

Since you are supervising this group of people, you will also have some control over the equipment and materials used by your work group. Thus, the concept of a cost center is to accumulate all of the costs associated with some logical organizational group. This allows supervisors to have some idea of the total costs involved with their groups. It also allows comparison with past cost data and inputs for budget estimates for the future.

The number and type of cost centers are usually determined by the accounting department. If a supervisor supervises eight employees doing similar work, it is one logical cost center. If a supervisor has twenty-six employees doing three categories of work, then three cost centers may be realistic. The accounting department must balance the advantage of the detailed cost information with the cost required to gather and process the extra cost-center data. In many companies, cost centers are the same as departments. In other companies, a department may have a number of cost centers.

In almost all organizations the cost-center concept is taken for granted. The cost-center concept can work, however, only if every single cost, regardless of how large or how small, is assigned to a cost center. By adding up all the cost centers of your organization you will have an accurate record of every penny spent by your company.

WAYS TO GATHER
ACTUAL COST DATA

The definition of a budget is an estimate of costs in the future. The budget cycle concept (introduced in Chapter 1 and discussed in detail in Chapter 7), notes, however, that most companies accumulate actual cost data for a given time period and compare actual costs with the budgeted costs. Any differences (variances) can then be investigated and explained by the supervisors and managers involved. In addition, the actual cost data for a time period are the normal starting base for future budgets. Thus, it is reasonable to discuss the ways in which actual costs are gathered at this point.

While cost measurement was discussed briefly in the preceding chapter, some specifics in the cost-center framework are worthwhile here. The cost-center data are no more accurate than the techniques used to gather the data. There are many ways that data are accumulated and assigned to a cost center. Generally, there is a well-established paperwork flow within the company from which cost data are collected.

For most companies, the major paperwork flow consists of forms for work orders, purchase orders, material requisitions, and time sheets. These four concepts are discussed below. Other forms are also used, such as expense-account forms and shipping documents. These forms are similar to the main four forms, and separate discussion is not necessary.

Work Order

Exhibit 4–3 shows a sample work order for our example company.

This work-order form includes all the information required by most companies. It is used to request maintenance work and capital-project work. Generally, the work-order form has pre-assigned numbers to avoid duplicate numbers. (Most companies keep track of the pre-assigned numbers. If you make an error on the form, void it and return it to accounting rather than throw it away.) On the form, you have a section for the requester to identify the work to be

EXHIBIT 4-3

Sample Work-Order Form

WORK ORDER
HARRISONBURG OFFICE EQUIPMENT
MANUFACTURING COMPANY

Requester   **Work-Order No.** _____

Dept. charged _____ Cost center charged _____
Work required, including justification _____

_____

_____

_____

_____

Equip. No. _____ Drawings attached? _____ Date wanted _____
Requested by _____ Date _____

Estimated Costs and Approvals

Labor $ _____

_____

Material $ _____

_____

Other $ _____

_____

Estimated by _____ Date _____
Reviewed by _____ Date _____
Approved by (1) _____ Date _____
Approved by (2) _____ Date _____

Maintenance

Repair code _____ Acc't'g code _____ Cost-center No. _____
Special instructions _____

_____

_____

Work completed: Date _____ Closed by _____

---

performed, and the department and cost center to be charged. You also have a section for cost estimates of carrying out the work and for any approvals necessary. (Most companies have an approval route that depends upon the amount of the work order; the larger the amount, the higher the level manager required to approve the work order.) This work-order form authorizes the work. After the work is completed, a copy of the form is sent to accounting to close out the work order. The actual charges against the work order, however, come from the employee time sheets, material requisitions, and purchase orders.

Purchase Order

A sample purchase-order form is shown in Exhibit 4–4. This form includes items on most company purchase orders. The form number is normally pre-assigned. Note that the requester is expected to fill the form out with as much information as possible, including the cost-center and work-order numbers. Many of the items, such as suggested vendor and F.O.B. (freight on board: the location where the buyer begins paying the freight), may not be known by the requester and can be added by purchasing. The appropriate signatures, again depending upon the amount of the order, are obtained. The purchase-order form is sent to purchasing, which places the order with an outside vendor. After receipt of the items, appropriate shipping charges may need to be added.

When all activity on the purchase order is complete, a copy of the form with the actual dollar amounts is sent to accounting for inclusion in the cost-center actual budget report. (If your company allows more than one item on a purchase order, each item may be charged to the cost center when it is received, rather than waiting for the entire purchase order to be completed.)

13

EXHIBIT 4-4

Sample Purchase-Order Form

PURCHASE ORDER
HARRISONBURG OFFICE EQUIPMENT
MANUFACTURING COMPANY

Purchase-Order No. _____

Quantity	Unit	Our Part No.	Description Includes Vendor Part Number	Unit Price	Total Price

Suggested vendor _____

Address _____

_____

Delivery requested _____ F.O.B. _____ Terms _____

Deliver to _____

Used on equipment _____

Requested by _____ Date _____

Approved by (1) _____ Date _____
Approved by (2) _____ Date _____

Cost-center No. _____ Acc't'g No. _____
Work-order No. _____
Special instructions _____
_____
_____

Order completed: Date _____ Closed by _____

Material Requisition

Material requisitions are used to withdraw production materials and operating supplies from the storeroom. The form
generally has pre-assigned numbers. The requester fills out
all items, and has it approved by the necessary managers.
Note that unit costs are not listed by the requester. The unit
costs are not really of concern to the individuals withdrawing
the material, since they must have the material to carry out
their work. The material-requisition form is turned into the
storeroom. When the order is filled, a copy is sent to accounting, which translates the material units into dollars and
charges the appropriate cost center. A sample form is shown
in Exhibit 4–5.

Time Sheets

Most employees turn in some record of the work they have
performed during the day. In some companies it may be
time cards on which employees clock in and out on specific
jobs. In other companies it may be filling out a time sheet
daily or weekly on which employees indicate what hours
they have worked on different activities. (Some companies
will use both: clock cards for hourly employees and time
sheets for salaried employees.) For supervisor and upper-

EXHIBIT 4-5

Sample Material-Requisition Form

MATERIAL REQUISITION
HARRISONBURG OFFICE EQUIPMENT
MANUFACTURING COMPANY

Requisition No. _____

Part Number	Quantity	Unit	Description

Date delivery requested _____

Deliver to _____

Requested by _____ Date _____

Approved by (1) _____ Date _____

Approved by (2) _____ Date _____

Cost-center No. _____ Acc't'g No._____

Work-order No. _____

Special instructions _____

_____

_____

Order Completed: Date _____ Closed by _____

level managers, 100 percent of their time may be automatically charged to a cost center by the accounting department without any additional paperwork being put through.

A sample time sheet for the Harrisonburg Office Equipment Manufacturing Company is shown in Exhibit 4–6.

Exhibit 4–6 is a daily time sheet filled out by all employees who are not supervisors or managers. Employees must list a description of all the work they performed, including a job code, cost center, and work code for the work. Each time sheet must total the number of hours the employee is to be paid, so non-productive time (illness, vacation, waiting for work) must be assigned to an indirect-labor job account code. These daily sheets are turned into accounting and used to charge back the costs against your cost center and against the job code and are also used for payroll purposes.

Other Actual
Cost-Data Gathering

Capital-equipment items are not charged directly to a cost center although they are largely under the control of the cost-center supervisor. Depreciation of the capital equipment is charged to the cost center on a periodic basis (monthly, quarterly, or yearly), even though the supervisor has no control over depreciation. The amount of depreciation is an accounting decision and will be discussed in more detail in later chapters.

Cost centers are set up for all organizational groups, not just production groups. That is, if you have a janitorial department, all costs for its activities will originally be assigned to the janitorial department. After these charges are accumulated for a time period, say a month, they will then be allocated to the cost centers for which the janitorial department actually did the work. In the same way, the maintenance department may accumulate all of its charges against a maintenance cost center but keep track of what depart-

EXHIBIT 4–6

Sample Employee Daily Time Sheet

EMPLOYEE DAILY TIME SHEET
HARRISONBURG OFFICE EQUIPMENT
MANUFACTURING COMPANY

Date: ＿＿＿＿＿

Employee: ＿＿＿＿＿＿＿＿＿＿ Employee No. ＿＿＿＿

Department: ＿＿＿＿＿＿＿＿＿＿＿ Shift ＿＿＿＿

Job Code	Cost Center	Work Code	Description	Hours

Total ＿＿＿＿＿＿＿＿＿＿＿＿＿＿＿＿＿

Approved by (1) ＿＿＿＿＿＿＿＿＿ Date ＿＿＿
Approved by (2) ＿＿＿＿＿＿＿＿＿ Date ＿＿＿

Acc't'g No. ＿＿＿＿＿＿
Special notes ＿＿＿＿＿＿＿＿＿＿＿＿＿＿
＿＿＿＿＿＿＿＿＿＿＿＿＿＿＿＿＿＿＿＿
＿＿＿＿＿＿＿＿＿＿＿＿＿＿＿＿＿＿＿＿

ments the maintenance center worked for. These costs will then be allocated back to these production departments at the end of the month.

Regardless of whether the costs remain with the cost center or are allocated to other cost centers, the key to the budgeting system is to make sure that every single cost gets charged to some cost center when the cost is incurred.

COST-CENTER BUDGET FORMAT

As with the other budget forms, the forms for cost centers will vary widely from company to company, and sometimes even differ for different departments within the same company. Exhibit 4 – 7 shows a cost-center budget form incorporating the most common cost components.

This form would be used by each department or cost center. The example shown is for the Partitions Department, Cost Center (Department) 14, for the month of October. Dollar amounts are listed for each cost item, but these are intended only to complete the budget form, not as examples of realistic costs. (A detailed explanation of how to estimate the costs for each line item for a new department is shown in Chapter 6.)

Across the top of the form are listed the column headings: the cost item itself, the units in which the cost item is expressed (if any), the quantity of the cost item (if appropriate), the unit cost of the cost item (if appropriate), and the total amount of that cost line.

Down the left side of the form is listed each cost category line by line. The lines are generally numbered with account numbers. Hence, this type of budget form is often called a "line item" budget. The line items shown here include costs the cost-center supervisor both can and cannot control. While the way supervisors respond to actual costs depends upon their degree of controllability, for budgeting

EXHIBIT 4–7

Cost-Center Budget

HARRISONBURG OFFICE EQUIPMENT
MANUFACTURING COMPANY
COST-CENTER BUDGET
COST CENTER 14, PARTITIONS DEPARTMENT
OCTOBER, 198x

Item	Unit	Quantity	Cost	Total
1.1 Hourly labor	hrs	1,437	$7.63	$10,964
1.2 Salaried labor				1,200
1.3 Overtime	hrs	52	14.90	775
1.4 Benefits				4,522
1.5 Repair labor	hrs	100	9.93	993
2.1 Repair materials				310
3.1 Misc.				471
4.1 Process supplies				2,140
5.1 Outside services				0
6.1 Utilities				320
7.1 Depreciation				2,710
8.1 Production materials:				
8.11 Wood				310
8.12 Metal				8,714
8.13 Other				1,574
9.1 Factory indirect-cost allocation				5,030
10.1 Total				$40,033

purposes they will be expected to include both types of costs on their cost-center forms.

The line items on Exhibit 4–7 are:

1.1 Hourly labor. Hourly labor is the cost of the hours of labor charged to this cost center by employees who directly produce the products. It would include piece-rate work if appropriate. It would include only the actual hours worked so that costs like vacations, sick leave, overtime, and fringe benefits would be charged to other line items. For the monthly actual cost report, hourly labor figures would be gathered from the daily time sheets of each employee and summarized by the accounting department.

1.2 Salaried labor. These costs are salaried employees charged to the cost center. Some individuals may have 100 percent of their time charged to one cost center, while others may have only a portion of their time charged to a single cost center. For both the budget and the monthly actual cost report, the percentage of each individual's salary from payroll records will be allocated to the cost center based upon the estimated percentage of time worked for that cost center.

1.3 Overtime. Overtime is the added amount above the normal rate paid to non-exempt employees for overtime in accordance with state and federal laws and company rules. (In general, those individuals not in supervisory or professional positions must be paid overtime.) Usually overtime is an additional 50 percent of the straight time rate for hours over eight in a day or forty in a week. (Sometimes company rules or union agreements require double time for Sunday or holiday work.) Since the regular wages are included in the hourly labor line, only the additional amount is listed on this overtime line. For the monthly actual cost report, overtime charges are picked up by the accounting department from the employee time sheets and are charged to the cost center.

1.4 Benefits. The salaries listed above do not include benefits, such as insurance, health care, and vacations. These are listed separately to identify clearly their costs. Two general methods of determining these benefit costs are used. In the first, the cost for vacations will be charged in the month in which the employee actually took time off for vacations. Costs for items like insurance and health care will be charged on a per person basis. In the second method, all benefit costs are estimated for a year and allocated to each cost center each month, generally on the basis of hourly labor hours. In either method, the information is supplied to the accounting department by the personnel department to make up the monthly actual-cost report.

1.5 Repair labor. Repair labor is labor hours the maintenance department has charged during the month to your cost center for work done to repair your equipment. It should not include maintenance work done by outside vendors, since this is charged to another account. (If you are the maintenance department, this would include only repair work on your own equipment. All of your regular hourly charges would be charged to your maintenance cost center as 1.1 Hourly Labor and then allocated to other cost centers.) For your monthly actual-cost report, the accounting department will gather this data from the time sheets of the maintenance personnel.

While it is not common, a few organizations may charge all repair costs to the maintenance department and then allocate all the charges to individual departments. Even if this is done, it will still show up on this line of your department cost-center report.

2.1 Repair materials. Repair materials are materials the maintenance department used in repairing items in your department. Even though they are indirect costs, they would generally be charged directly to your cost center and not reallocated from the maintenance department. Repair materials would be taken out of inventory with a materials requisition. A copy of the requisition would go to the accounting department for summary on your monthly actual-budget report.

3.1 Miscellaneous. Miscellaneous includes all of the small items not appropriate for other lines and not large enough to justify a separate line for most departments. This could include items like stationary supplies, instrument cal-ibration, and travel expenses. Actual charges would reach the accounting department on purchase orders, material requisitions, employee time sheets, and travel report forms. The charges would then be assigned to the cost-center monthly actual-cost report.

4.1 Process supplies. Process supplies are the supplies that are used directly in producing the work. They could include lubricants for equipment, tools, shop rags, and gloves. In non-manufacturing cost centers, process supplies could be very small, and in fact this line item could even be omitted for those departments. Process supplies would be withdrawn from inventory with a material requisition that would include a cost-center number for the accounting department to use in the monthly actual-cost report.

5.1 Outside services. Outside services would include items like consultants' fees, equipment repair, or maintenance work done by outside vendors, and outside training courses. The actual costs for these items would come direct from purchase orders.

6.1 Utilities. Utilities include items like heat, light, electricity, and steam. Utilities could also include rented space used only by your department. If utility charges can be determined separately for your cost center, they should be charged directly to your cost center. Many utility charges, however, cannot be measured separately for each cost center. For these cases, the utility costs are charged to a utility-department cost center and then allocated to other cost centers based upon some consistent measure, such as the cost center's square footage compared to that of the plant as a whole. Again, regardless of how the utility costs are determined they will be listed on this line.

7.1 Depreciation. Depreciation is the way in which the cost of the cost center's capital equipment is written off against operating cost each month. The amount of depreciation charged each month is an accounting decision over which supervisors have no control. Nevertheless, it is a legitimate cost of the cost center and is listed on the cost center's monthly actual-cost report by the accounting department.

8.1 Production materials. Production materials are the raw materials used directly in producing the products and services that you produce. For our Harrisonburg Office Equipment Manufacturing Company example, these are broken down into sub-categories of 8.11, Wood, 8.12, Metal, and 8.13, Other. This is because the major ingredients used to produce the office equipment products are metal, wood, and other materials. For the monthly actual-cost report, the units of materials and dollar figures for these line items would be taken from the forms used to withdraw the material from inventory. For a non-manufacturing cost center, production materials might be negligible, and these line items could be omitted if desired.

9.1 Factory indirect-cost allocation. Factory indirect-cost allocation is the portion of other factory expenses that go to support the cost center. This would include items like the factory manager's salary, the security force, the shipping and receiving department, and secretarial help.

It would not include sales department costs and accounting costs since these would not be factory costs and would be charged to cost centers outside the manufacturing department. The cost-center supervisor will have no control over these indirect allocated items, but they are legitimate expenses to support the cost center and should be listed on the cost-center monthly budget. Factory indirect costs can be allocated from other cost centers in a number of ways, such as production volume, total labor hours, or total cost-center budget. In any case, the decisions on factory indirect-cost allocation will be made by upper-level management and listed by the accounting department on the monthly actual-cost report.

10.1 Total.   Total is the sum of the different line items for the cost center.

In Chapter 6, we will use this operating cost-center budget framework for developing the first budget for a new department cost center. In Chapter 8, we will provide details in using this budget framework to develop and revise budgets for already existing cost centers.

5

COST SYSTEMS

*"What are cost systems and
how are they used in budgeting?"*

PURPOSES OF A
COST-ACCOUNTING SYSTEM

In order to provide data for use by operating managers, a company must organize a cost-accounting system designed to gather actual cost data. This cost data is important since it may be used in developing future budgets and can be used to measure the cost of products produced. One of your responsibilities as a supervisor or manager is to see that cost data gathered is as accurate as possible. This cost-accounting system is designed for use within the firm and is not intended for stockholder or other external uses. Cost-accounting systems may also be called managerial accounting systems.

A cost-accounting system has a number of specific uses within the firm. One use is to determine costs in a specific time period in order to calculate the cost of products sold (as a component in determining profit) and in the valuation of inventory.

A second use of cost accounting is to provide data for use in budgeting, cost control and cost minimization. Past cost figures are frequently employed in developing operating budgets. Actual costs can then be compared with the estimated (budgeted) costs as an element of cost control. By determining where costs are currently occurring on an accurate basis, the foundation is laid for an analysis of where costs can be decreased.

A third major purpose of the cost-accounting system is to provide a basis for management decisions. While not all decisions are made on the basis of cost alone, all management decisions should be made with a clear picture of costs involved in implementing any decision.

A fourth use of a cost-accounting system is to provide an audit trail. All sources of revenue and costs within the company must be clearly documented through a system of purchase orders, invoices, checks, and other documents. Such documentation is necessary so that auditors (and managers) can check back on revenue and costs to see that no fraud has occurred. For this reason you must be careful not to destroy numbered documents such as purchase orders since they will form part of the audit trail. The system is followed by both internal and external auditors to verify costs.

Finally, the cost-accounting system allows calculation of the unit cost of products sold as an element in the pricing decision. Although price is not controlled totally by cost, since competitive and market factors are involved, an accurate knowledge of costs is necessary to insure that in the long run the revenues from sales do cover all costs and provide a profit.

In developing a cost-accounting system, different methods may be used in determining product costs, in collecting costs, and in determining the valuation techniques to be employed in reporting costs. You will need to become familiar with some of the different methods employed in collecting and reporting costs in order to understand cost control and other internal reports provided for your use. As an operating manager or supervisor, you may also be in a position to evaluate the effectiveness of the techniques used in collecting costs in your department. You may be in a position to suggest modifications based upon your observations at the department level.

ACCOUNTING SYSTEMS

There are two basic types of accounting systems: cash and accrual.

A cash system reports revenue and costs as the actual cash (bills and checks) is received and spent. This system is followed by most individuals and by some small companies. The most common record-keeping system is a checkbook, where the current balance measures the financial health of the individual or the firm.

Most medium-size and large companies use the accrual system. In this system, revenue is listed when it is earned, i.e., when the finished products are sold. Whether the cash actually is received in that month or in future months does not matter. Costs are also listed when they occur, even if they are not actually paid until later. This is done so that we can "match" revenues with the costs which were incurred in producing that revenue. We must know how much it cost to produce a product in order to set a price and to calculate our profit on the sale. The accrual system is used because it allows management to judge more accurately the success of operations in a given time period.

Even using the accrual system, most firms keep three sets of accounting records. One set is consistent with tax laws and is used for tax reporting. Another set is what the board of directors feels is the most accurate and is used for stockholder reporting. The third is for internal management control (cost-accounting or managerial-accounting system). Keeping three sets of books is perfectly legal, providing the purpose of each is clearly specified.

PROCESS-COST SYSTEM
VERSUS JOB-COST SYSTEM

In general, there are two basic types of cost-accounting techniques used for collecting costs: job cost and process cost.

Job-Order Cost System

A job-order cost system is used where the products produced can be clearly separated into individual units (or group of units). Examples would include building a house, building a large pump, or building a piece of specialty furniture. The key feature of job-order cost accounting is that cost data is kept for each job, and the exact costs incurred on that job are recorded and accumulated into a total job cost. The result is a total cost figure for a specific job.

In a manufacturing operation, total planned output for a month might be divided into a number of job lots. A job-order number would be assigned to each lot. For example, if our goal was to manufacture 4,000 units in one month, we might set up each 500 units as a job order. Actual costs would be collected for each job by assigning costs not only to a cost center but to a job order as well. In this way we can accumulate the total costs per group of 500 units, and could compute an average cost per unit on each job order. As a supervisor or manager, you will be expected to evaluate the average unit cost for each job order to see if costs are out of line with the expected costs. Periodically (monthly or quarterly), the accounting department will compute an average cost for all of the units produced by combining the average costs of each job order. This periodic average should also be scrutinized to see that average unit cost is within expected limits.

In our Harrisonburg Office Equipment Manufacturing Company, for example, a group of products (part of a month's output) would be considered a job and assigned a job-order number. All costs would be charged to this number (as well as to a cost center), whether the work was done in one department or many departments.

Process-Cost System

A process-cost accounting system is used where products are being manufactured on a more or less continuous schedule. Here it is not possible to assign costs directly to a specific unit of output, since the unit of output is either not a single, discrete physical unit or cannot be broken down into small groups for the collection of cost figures. Examples would be costs for a sewage-treatment plant, a paper mill, or an oil refinery. Because of the difficulty of assigning costs to a specific unit, costs are accumulated for a period of time, say a month. This total monthly cost is then divided by the number of product units produced to get an average cost per unit.

In general, the costing system that should be used is determined by considering the products to be produced. Where either system could be used, the easier and cheaper process-cost accounting system is preferred. A company may employ both systems. Job-order accounting, for example, might be used for specific project work or construction, while process-cost accounting could be used for manufacturing operations.

ABSORPTION COSTING
VERSUS DIRECT COSTING

In a cost-accounting system different methods may be used in determining what costs are to be charged against a particular job order or product, and cost center. These methods include absorption costing and direct costing.

In absorption (full) costing all costs (variable, semi-variable, and fixed costs) are collected and reported as costs associated with a particular product or job order (as well as being assigned to a cost center). Absorption costing is designed to reflect all of the costs required for the manufacture of a product. Under an absorption costing system, your cost-center budget may include fixed costs, such as depreciation. The cost-center budget form in Exhibit 4–7 is a budget developed under an absorption costing system.

In direct (variable) costing only those variable and semi-variable costs which are directly associated with the manufacture of a product are reported. Variable costs would include direct labor and direct materials. Some examples of semi-variable costs would be overtime, benefits, repair labor, repair materials, and process supplies. Companies may vary in their definitions of semi-variable costs to be included. When a direct-costing system is used, costs need to be identified clearly as either fixed, variable, or semi-variable costs.

Absorption (full) costing is frequently used in conjunction with fixed budgets, which are not readjusted to reflect actual output during a given budget period. You will find wide variations in costing systems and type of budgets employed, however. Indeed, companies may use different combinations of costing systems (absorption and direct) and types of budgets (fixed and flexible) within the same organization. In any case, you as a supervisor or manager should be familiar with the type of costing system employed. Your supervisor or budget director can be helpful in providing answers to any questions you might have.

THE BUDGET
AS A COMPARISON TOOL

The most sophisticated accounting system has no meaning in and of itself. Accounting data can provide the basis for practical managerial tools, however. For example, two methods are generally used in developing an operating budget. In the first, past cost figures are used in developing the new budget. In the second, standard figures, usually developed using industrial engineering techniques, are used in figuring number of labor hours, quantity of materials, and other estimates needed to develop the budget.

Once the budget has been developed and approved it will in turn serve as a comparison base against which actual costs will be evaluated. This comparison of budget figures (expected costs) against those costs actually incurred in a given time period is an important element in your company's cost-control procedures. That is, the costs incurred by a department in a month have meaning only if they can be compared to something. The important question is not about the necessity of comparison, but about what data base current costs should be compared against.

There are a number of potential comparison bases. As we have said, one is an ideal cost, often called a standard cost. A second is data collected from your own department's past history. Many others are, of course, possible.

Standard Costs

Standard-cost systems are widely used. In a standard-cost system, the costs for a department are estimated on the basis that everything will run smoothly. Labor costs are estimated based upon some time standard, materials costs upon studied quantity estimates, and other costs upon ideal support costs. Standard costs may be used in actually developing a budget. In using a standard-cost system in developing a budget, some "ideal" cost figure or standard would be used in determining the labor hours and materials, both direct and indirect, needed to produce a particular volume of output. Standard costs are developed by applying industrial engineering techniques, such as time-and-motion studies, to tasks to be performed. These studies provide an efficiency target against which actual performance can be evaluated. Standard costs can be adjusted statistically from a theoretical base to take into account practical problems.

The basic theory of standard costs suggests that once they are set they are changed infrequently. (They can be changed for clear-cut reasons, like wage increases due to contract negotiations or changes in raw material or energy prices.) There is a significant problem in keeping standard costs realistic, and a great deal of time and money can be spent just trying to keep standard costs up-to-date. Yet, if standard costs are not realistic, supervisors and managers will consider them of little value and they will not serve the purpose of effective cost control. In many cases, the cost of trying to keep a standard-cost system up-to-date and useful has been greater than the value gained from the standard-cost system.

Past Cost History

Use of actual costs developed from your company's past performance can provide another budgeting base. This method has its strengths and weaknesses as well. One of the major weaknesses is that you are assuming the costs you have incurred in the past are in fact reasonable costs. Another weakness is that, in the United States' economic system, prices, and of course costs, have been rising over the last few decades. Thus, comparisons to past history will almost always show higher costs today.

The strengths of this system, however, often overshadow these weaknesses. If your firm's past operations have been relatively efficient, your past costs may be a good base for comparison. Using fairly recent past costs also means the data is relatively up-to-date. In addition, the cost of gathering and analyzing the cost data may be quicker and cheaper using past history as a base. One system which has been employed by many firms compares the costs of a department for a particular month to the average costs per month of the department for the fiscal year to date. That is, June's actual expenses are compared to a budget that is the average actual expenses of January through May. Thus, the costs going into the comparison base are never more than twelve months old. (This system assumes that production each month is relatively constant.)

As a supervisor or manager, you will need to know what type of cost-comparison method is used in your company. You will also need to find out how the comparison base is calculated.

VARIANCES

When using either a standard-cost system or past history, by comparing the actual cost data for a month against the expected budgets, any differences can be seen. These differences are called "variances" from the expected costs. Variances should be closely watched by management, since they identify areas where actual costs were different from expected costs. Individual managers responsible for each department should be asked to investigate the reasons for each large variance, and to take steps to control such variances in the future. The concept of variance analysis is one of the cornerstones of a sound cost-control system. Managers should want to know why their operations differed from what was expected, and a variance report and analysis identify the areas to investigate. Variance analysis will be discussed further in Chapter 7.

COST-VOLUME-PROFIT
RELATIONSHIPS

As was stated earlier, management needs information on costs and sales in order to make intelligent business decisions in both long-range and short-term planning. For example, shall production of a product line be expanded, maintained at current level, or discontinued? Should sales territories be expanded, maintained at the current level, or discontinued? Should a special job order be accepted?

The application of cost-volume-profit (break-even) techniques is a useful tool to provide data for managers in making such decisions. Cost-volume-profit techniques can be used with historical data or with future estimates of costs and sales data. These techniques require that costs be broken down into variable (includes variable and semi-variable) costs and fixed costs so that the impact of changes in fixed costs, variable costs, and sales quantities, price, and mix on the profits of the firm can be analyzed.

You need to be familiar with the concepts involved in cost-volume-profit analyses. You may be called upon to supply cost information in the form of estimates for labor needs under current production demands or with other costs associated with variable and semi-variable costs under your control. Cost-volume-profit relationships can impact upon budget decisions at all levels of management.

Break-Even Analysis

The area of cost-volume-profit relationships deals with changes of quantity of production and its subsequent effect on costs and profits. The area is often called break-even analysis, defining break-even as the point of zero profit, the volume of sales where total revenues and total costs are equal.

While the break-even analysis can be expressed in a number of ways, the most basic formula is:

Profit = sales revenue − variable costs − fixed costs,

where sales revenue is defined as selling price times quantity sold.

If we set profit equal to zero, then the break-even point is the quantity sold where total revenue equals total costs:

Sales revenue = variable costs + fixed costs

Of course, few companies deliberately aim for zero profit. However, the break-even formula can also show the expected profit at a particular level of sales, or the volume of sales necessary to provide a particular profit.

The concept of break-even is most easily shown on a graph, such as Exhibit 5–1.

In Exhibit 5–1, fixed costs are shown as a horizontal line, constant over the quantity range of 0 to 4,000 units. Variable costs (includes semi-variable costs) are zero at zero units of output, and increase at a constant rate per unit as output increases. Adding fixed and variable costs graphically gives the total-cost line. Revenue at zero units of sales is zero. The total-revenue line increases at a constant rate, the average unit selling price. The point where the total-revenue line crosses the total-cost line is the break-even point, the point where all costs are covered.

Contribution Margin Technique

A second important break-even method is the contribution margin or marginal income technique. If you remember, your company has certain fixed costs which must be allocated across cost centers. Any money made by a cost center over and above that center's variable costs (includes variable and semi-variable costs) can be used to cover fixed costs. Once all costs have been paid, then a profit will be shown on the books. Profit centers which do not appear to be highly profitable may still be economically valuable to the firm by their contribution toward payment of total fixed costs for the firm.

Contribution margin is the difference between sales rev-

EXHIBIT 5–1

Break-even Analysis

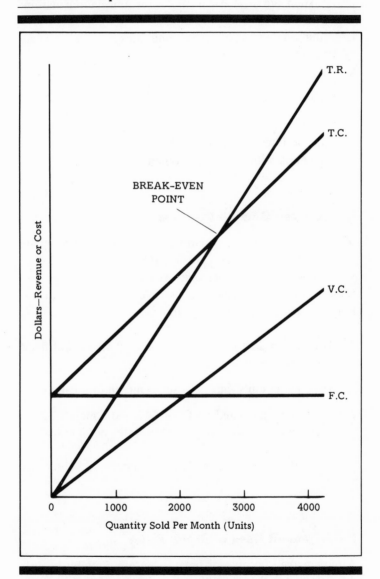

enue and variable costs. Any sales revenue above the variable costs contributes to paying for the fixed costs and to profit. There are two basic formulas for contribution margin:

Contribution margin per unit = unit sales price − unit variable costs

$$\text{Break-even in units} = \frac{\text{Fixed costs}}{\text{Contribution margin per unit}}$$

The best way to show both contribution margin and break-even is with a sample problem.

Break-Even Sample Problem

You are supervisor of a department producing one complete product. Your fixed costs are $68,000 per month and your variable costs are $38 per unit. You produce only for customer orders (no finished-goods inventory), and your average selling price is $94 per unit.

1. How much does each unit sold contribute toward fixed costs and profit?

2. How many units must you sell a month to break even?

3. To achieve a desired profit of $45,000 a month before taxes, what should your monthly sales be in units?

Work this problem out. The calculations are shown in Exhibit 5–2.

Management Uses of Break-Even

Although the concepts of break-even are straightforward, they illustrate a thought pattern that is particularly important

EXHIBIT 5-2

Break-even Sample-Problem Solution

Sample-Problem Solution

1. Contribution margin = unit sales price − unit variable cost
Contribution margin = $94 − 38 = $56

2. Profit = sales revenue − variable costs − fixed costs
$0 = 94\,Q − 38\,Q − 68,000$
$Q = \dfrac{68,000}{56} = 1,214$ units per month

3. Profit = sales revenue − variable costs − fixed costs
$45,000 = 94\,Q − 38\,Q − 68,000$
$Q = \dfrac{113,000}{56} = 2,018$ units per month

GRAPHICALLY,

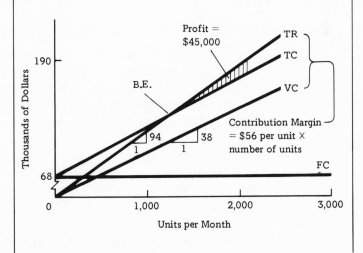

in operating supervisors and managers. By this type of analysis, helpful information is gained for making decisions on items like pricing, new equipment purchases, and reducing production versus building finished-goods inventory.

If your company is one that uses large amounts of plant and equipment, your fixed costs are high. Thus, the contribution concept is particularly important. At the break-even volume, all fixed costs are covered. Every additional unit of output will then make a larger contribution to profit.

If you are working in a continuous-process company, downtime is also particularly important. Lost production due to downtime may never be recovered. At best, the fixed costs are spread over fewer units, average total costs per unit go up, and profit declines.

INVENTORY POLICIES

The purpose of inventories is to support the production and sales departments so that uneven flows in one department will not affect the other. For example, if the production department should experience a temporary work stoppage, the sales department can continue to supply customers with units from the finished-goods inventory. On the other hand if sales should experience a temporary slump, management may choose not to disrupt production schedules. One way of doing this is to allow the finished-goods inventory to expand.

Your company will maintain three different types of inventory: (1) raw-materials inventory, (2) work-in-process inventory, and (3) finished-goods inventory. These inventories are considered assets of the firm and will appear as assets on the balance-sheet financial statement. There are costs associated with inventory, however. Money used to purchase raw materials, for example, is not available to the firm for other purposes. Finished goods held in inventory are not contributing revenue through sales. Some other costs, associated with all types of inventory, would include costs of storage and insurance. Inventories may also become obsolete. If a product line is discontinued, the company may have to dispose of inventories at a loss or at a very low rate of return on investment. If the manufacturing process is changed, current raw-materials inventory may become obsolete with similar results.

Inventory management may become a source of conflict between the sales, manufacturing, and finance departments. The sales department would like large inventories of finished goods to meet customers' demands and to allow for prompt delivery of orders. The manufacturing department would like large inventories of raw materials to ensure ready availability of raw materials for the manufacturing process. The finance department would like to keep all inventories to a minimum in order to minimize the costs associated with inventory. The company must try to minimize costs associated with carrying too much inventory or not carrying enough (lost sales, production slowdowns). For this reason, management will establish inventory policies and procedures.

One consequence of rising interest rates is that companies have an incentive to cut back on inventories at every level. Since many companies have to borrow money to pay for their inventory, the same inventory at higher interest costs more. This higher interest is a direct drain on profits.

ECONOMICAL ORDER QUANTITY (EOQ)

One method which management may use for determining inventory levels is a formal mathematical calculation, called the economical order quantity (EOQ). The economical-order-quantity concept shows a way of looking at the effect of interest on inventory level.

$$EOQ = \sqrt{2FU/CP}$$

where EOQ is the optimum quantity to be ordered, F is the cost of placing and receiving an order, U is the annual estimated usage in units, C is the carrying costs expressed as a percentage of inventory value, and P is the purchase price per unit of inventory.

The interest paid for money to carry inventory is a component of the carrying cost C. As C increases, the optimum quantity that should be purchased decreases. In a few cases, this simply means more frequent reorders; in most cases, the result is a reduction in total inventory. Of course, one method to overcome a rise in interest rates is to decrease the purchase price P. This, however, is a direct profit drain on the seller.

If any company is truly interested in minimizing the total costs of ordering and carrying inventory, it will decrease inventory as carrying costs increase. This is, of course, what has been happening in recent years to the United States economy in general.

Inventory decisions must be made before operating budgets can be calculated. These decisions may influence costs, production schedules, and quantities of output to be produced. You will need to be aware of any changes in inventory policy if you are to budget effectively. In addition, you need to bring to your supervisor's attention any adverse changes in your department which may be caused by current or future inventory problems.

INVENTORY PROCEDURES

We have discussed inventory procedures in earlier chapters. Your company will have specific procedures (paperwork flow) to be followed for withdrawing raw materials from inventory. You should know what procedures are to be followed. In addition, your company will have set up procedures for reordering raw materials and other stores. Today, most companies have computerized their inventories, so that additions and withdrawals are automatically entered on the inventory records. For raw materials and other stores, each type of material will have an automatic reorder point. When a certain supply level is reached (reorder point), purchasing will place an order with the suppliers for further stock in that item. If reorder points are set too low, you may experience difficulty in obtaining the production materials you need. It is a good idea for you to keep an eye on present inventory levels to be sure that materials will be available when you need them. Again, if you are having problems, be sure to inform your supervisor immediately. You may also want to be on the lookout for changes in the quality of materials you are receiving through the purchasing department. Purchasing may order new materials from a different supplier in order to save on material costs. As a production supervisor, you may find that these cost savings are lost due to increased scrap costs from using inferior quality raw materials or stores. Again, be sure to bring such problems to the attention of your supervisor. These types of problems will have a direct impact on your own departmental budget.

PART II

OPERATING BUDGETS

NEW-DEPARTMENT
BUDGETING

*"How do you set up the original budget
for a new department?"*

INTRODUCTION

Today is July 1. You were put in charge of your new department last February, and since then you have been working with engineering to order the correct equipment and to
lay out the department. You are scheduled to be in operation
by October 1. Your supervisor stopped by to review your
plans and suggested that you ought to begin work on your
operating budget for the October through December quarter
and for the next year. You've been so involved in setting
up the new department that you never really thought about
the department's monthly budget.

Let us assume that the Harrisonburg Office Equipment
Manufacturing Company is adding a new department to
manufacture tables for computers and computer printers.
All of the machining, assembling, and finishing work on
these products will be done in the new department since
there is no capacity in the rest of the factory to produce
them. All other required work (like inventory storage, pack-

aging, and shipping) can be carried out in existing departments. The products, when the new department first starts up, will include a metal computer table (Product T-11), a wood computer table (Product T-12), a metal printer table (Product T-13), and a wood printer table (Product T-14). The four models are designed to accommodate microcomputers both for use at work and in the home. The printer table and the computer table will accommodate almost all models currently on the market and planned.

How would you go about setting up a monthly operating budget for your new department?

PLANNING THE BUDGET PROCESS

Since you are starting up a new department, you will have no detailed past history to guide you. You must then use a standard-cost system. The best way to develop the new standard-cost budget is to follow a consistent plan. Consider a set of steps like this:

1. Identify the company's and department's goals and objectives.

2. Determine the quantity of products to be produced by the department.

3. Based on this work load, estimate the manpower needed and the skills needed.

4. Estimate the material needed and its cost.

5. Estimate the other operating costs based upon the work load, manpower, and materials estimates using a departmental budget format like those listed earlier.

6. Develop a tentative budget.

7. Discuss it with your supervisor, the engineering people, and the accounting department, and revise it according to their suggestions.

CARRYING OUT
THE BUDGET PROCESS

Goals and Objectives

As the first step, you must understand your company's goals and objectives. Your company's goals and objectives may not help you much in the day-to-day management of your new department, but understanding them will help you make sure that what you are doing is what the company wants. All companies have goals and objectives even if they are not clearly stated. While company goals and objectives were discussed earlier, as a minimum you might expect: (1) a goal dealing with the amount of profit; (2) a goal dealing with marketing, such as market share; (3) another goal dealing with the desire for new products; (4) and perhaps an unstated goal about the desire for long-term existence of the company.

Of more importance, however, are the goals and objectives of your new department. The obvious objective will be the amount of work desired when the new department begins. Yet a new department is not designed for the amount of work expected when it first starts up. You must have some idea of what is expected over the next few years in terms of quantity of production. You must also have some idea of the quality level desired of the products to be produced. Are the products to be of high quality, with cost of secondary importance? Or is your target market the low end of a product line, where low price and hence low costs are more important than the highest quality level?

Of course for your department, profit goals may not be

stated. In fact profit requires knowledge of the selling price, and you will generally not have control over that. For an operating manager and an operating budget the profit component at the company level translates into cost control at the cost center or department level. That is, your goal should be to produce the products at the lowest cost consistent with the desired quality level and desired delivery schedule.

You may not know these goals and objectives right off. When in doubt ask your supervisor. Don't be surprised if your supervisor doesn't know the answers to your questions or if you are told formal objectives have not been defined. You can generally get enough information to help you make up your own mind, even if it is not as specific and formal as you might like it.

Let's look at our Harrisonburg Office Equipment Manufacturing Company. You've gone to your supervisor, and your supervisor has said the company's objectives are to make money. As the two of you start discussing it in more detail, some goals become clearer. First, the company was founded in 1869 just after the War and has made a reasonable profit ever since. The clear assumption is that it is going to be in business a very long time. Secondly, the company does most of its sales within a surrounding four-state region. While it is willing to sell anyplace, transportation costs, paid by the customer, make it more practical for the sales force to concentrate on customers within 300 miles of the factory. This area includes two large cities, and your supervisor feels that you have a good solid 20 percent of the market in this area. Thirdly, the company regularly adds new products to its product line, as long as they are consistent with current products. Finally, the general company products are aimed at the middle price range of the office equipment and furniture market. The company does not make the most expensive items, nor does it aim to compete in the very low-priced office furniture market.

This means that in considering goals and objectives in

your department, you must hit a balance between quality and cost. A good quality, particularly in terms of appearance, will aid sales. It must also be remembered that some of your customers will be shopping at office furniture stores for computer tables for their homes. This means that they might look at appearance and quality in a different way than if they were purchasing it for an office.

In determining the equipment requirements and plant layout for your new department, your management used a long range estimate of 3,200 units per month as the basis for calculations. They hoped to reach this amount in two years, and estimated that this would give them about the same 20 percent of the market as their other products.

Work Load Estimating

The starting point for your October-to-December budget is the output expected from your department. The most useful form to you is in terms of units of output expected. These estimates should be actual production required for these months, not the long-term expectations. If you don't know the work load expected, ask your supervisor or the sales department. We are assuming your new department will produce a number of products and that the date the products are required may not be uniform throughout the month. If this is the case, make sure that you know when during the month the different finished products will be desired. While the budget produced will be a monthly budget, the work load requirements may not be spread evenly over the month, and you may need to include estimates for overtime if schedule dates must be met. Generally, you will have no problem finding out how much work is required. Budgeting the costs to produce the output is more difficult.

For the Harrisonburg Office Equipment Manufacturing Company example, you talked to the sales department and the production scheduling department and they told you for

October to produce 400 metal printer tables, 400 wood printer tables, 400 metal computer tables, and 400 wood computer tables. (All of these units are shipped fully assembled.) This production is 50 percent of the capacity for which your new department was planned.

These units are required in inventory at the end of October, so production can be arranged throughout the month as you desire.

Rough sketches of the metal and wood computer tables are shown in Exhibit 6–2, and sketches of the metal and wood printer tables are shown in Exhibit 6–1.

Exhibits 6–1 and 6–2 are a simplification of engineering drawings for the computer table and the printer table. These drawings are the starting point for the manpower and material calculations you will need to make. Even if these calculations are actually made for you by the engineering department, you should understand the drawings so you can follow the way in which your budget is built from these basics.

Manpower and Skills Estimating

Manpower and labor skills estimating involves two activities: (1) estimating the labor hours of each job skill required, and (2) translating these estimates into the actual number of employees required.

Manpower skills estimating. If you're lucky, you will have an engineering department to do the detailed calculations of labor hours for you. If not, you'll have to do them yourself. In any case, these calculations are important numbers on which your budget is based, and you should understand how they are derived.

Let's assume your industrial engineering department will have developed the sequencing of operations required to manufacture your new products. The I.E. department will

EXHIBIT 6–1

Drawing of Printer Table
T–13 Metal   T–14 Wood

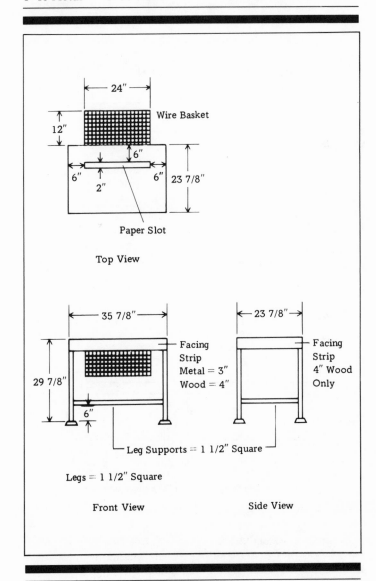

24″

Wire Basket

12″

6″

6″   6″   23 7/8″

2″

Paper Slot

Top View

35 7/8″   23 7/8″

Facing
Strip
Metal = 3″
Wood = 4″

Facing
Strip
4″ Wood
Only

29 7/8″

6″

Leg Supports = 1 1/2″ Square

Legs = 1 1/2″ Square

Front View   Side View

EXHIBIT 6-2

Drawing of Computer Table
T–11 Metal   T–12 Wood

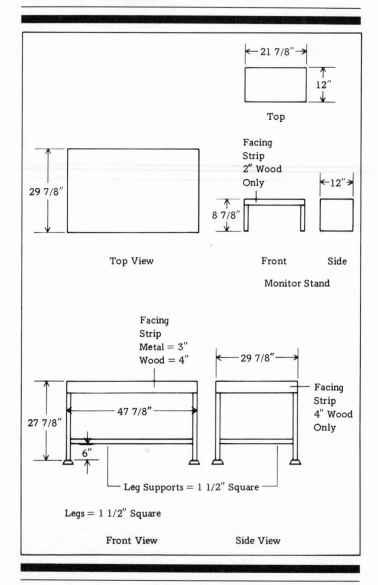

also have estimated the labor hours required for each operation to produce a unit of output. What you have to do is to take each labor component of each operation and multiply it by the units to be produced. Adding these numbers together will give you an estimate of the total labor hours required. Of more use than this total labor-hour figure, however, are the labor hours for each particular type of skill needed. Part of this calculation depends upon your company rules. That is, can people work only at certain duties and not do other duties, or could one person do multiple duties? For example, must a material handler move the material from machine to machine, or can the machine operator move the material after the work is complete?

You must add up the labor hours required for each different skill within your department because different skills will be paid at different rates. In general, the estimate of manpower on your budget will be in labor hours.

As an example, Exhibits 6–3 through 6–6 show the manufacturing operations and labor-hour estimates for the four products of this new department of the Harrisonburg Office Equipment Manufacturing Company.

The industrial engineering department has broken the labor skills down into four categories: (1) machinist, (2) laborer, (3) assembler, and (4) finisher. For each part of each table they have estimated the labor hours needed for each skill. By adding the labor hours for each part by skill, they can estimate the total labor hours required of each skill to produce each unit. For example, from Exhibit 6–3, for the metal computer table, product T-11, .15 hour of machinist time are estimated to machine the four legs, .10 hour to machine the leg supports, .46 hour to machine the top, and .19 hour to machine the monitor stand, giving a total machinist time of .90 hour per unit. In a similar fashion, the times for assemblers and finishers are calculated. Note that these time estimates include a 25 percent allowance for items like personal time of the employees, fatigue, and running out of work.

EXHIBIT 6-3

Manufacturing Operations and Labor Hours, Product T-11

HARRISONBURG OFFICE EQUIPMENT
MANUFACTURING COMPANY
MANUFACTURING OPERATIONS AND LABOR HOURS
PRODUCT T-11, METAL COMPUTER TABLE

Operation	Machinist Time
1. Legs—cut, drill, deburr	.15 hr/unit
2. Leg supports—cut, drill, deburr	.10
3. Top—cut, drill, deburr, form edges	.46
4. Monitor stand—cut, deburr, form	.19
5. Feet—purchased	0
Total	.90

Operation	Assembler Time
1. Attach legs to top	.28 hr/unit
2. Attach leg supports to legs	.08
3. Attach feet	.04
Total	.40

Operation	Finisher Time
1. Electrostatic paint	.53 hr/unit
2. Bake	.12
3. Inspect	.05
Total	.70

All times include 25% for personal allowance, rework, etc.

EXHIBIT 6-4

Manufacturing Operations and Labor Hours, Product T-12

HARRISONBURG OFFICE EQUIPMENT
MANUFACTURING COMPANY
MANUFACTURING OPERATIONS AND LABOR HOURS
PRODUCT T-12, WOOD COMPUTER TABLE

Operation	Machinist Time
1. Legs—cut, drill, deburr	.13 hr/unit
2. Leg supports—cut, drill, deburr	.07
3. Top—cut, deburr	.19
4. Facing strip—cut, deburr	.19
5. Monitor stand—cut, deburr	.12
6. Monitor stand supports—cut, deburr	.10
7. Feet—purchased	0
Total	.80

Operation	Assembler Time
1. Glue facing strips to top	.10 hr/unit
2. Attach legs to top/facing strips	.20
3. Attach leg supports to legs	.06
4. Attach feet	.04
5. Glue monitor stand pieces together	.09
6. Glue monitor stand supports in place	.11
Total	.60

Operation	Finisher Time
1. Stain edges, cut surfaces, touch up, etc.	.22 hrs/unit
2. Varnish	.33
3. Inspect	.05
Total	.60

All times include 25% for personal allowance, rework, etc.

EXHIBIT 6–5

Manufacturing Operations and Labor Hours, Product T–13

HARRISONBURG OFFICE EQUIPMENT
MANUFACTURING COMPANY
MANUFACTURING OPERATIONS AND LABOR HOURS
PRODUCT T–13, METAL PRINTER TABLE

Operation	Machinist Time
1. Legs—cut, drill, deburr	.18 hr/unit
2. Leg supports—cut, drill, deburr	.12
3. Top—cut, drill, cut slot, deburr, form edges	.70
4. Feet—purchased	0
5. Paper basket—purchased	0
Total	1.00

Operation	Assembler Time
1. Attach legs to top	.28 hr/unit
2. Attach leg supports to legs	.08
3. Attach feet	.04
Total	.40

Operation	Finisher Time
1. Electrostatic paint	.53 hr/unit
2. Bake	.12
3. Inspect	.05
Total	.70

All times include 25% for personal allowance, rework, etc.

EXHIBIT 6-6

Manufacturing Operations and Labor Hours Product T-14

HARRISONBURG OFFICE EQUIPMENT
MANUFACTURING COMPANY
MANUFACTURING OPERATIONS AND LABOR HOURS
PRODUCT T-14, WOOD PRINTER TABLE

Operation	Machinist Time
1. Legs—cut, drill, deburr	.13 hr/unit
2. Leg supports—cut, drill, deburr	.07
3. Top—cut, cut slot, deburr	.31
4. Facing strip—cut, drill, deburr	.19
5. Feet—purchased	0
6. Paper basket—purchased	0
Total	.70

Operation	Assembler Time
1. Glue facing strips to top	.10 hr/unit
2. Attach legs to top/facing strips	.20
3. Attach leg supports to legs	.06
4. Attach feet	.04
Total	.40

Operation	Finisher Time
1. Stain edges, cut surfaces, touch up, etc.	.22 hr/unit
2. Varnish	.33
3. Inspect	.05
Total	.60

All times include 25% for personal allowance, rework, etc.

You must then combine these individual unit labor hours into a department total, and multiply by the wage rate of each skill to arrive at the final budget.

Exhibit 6–7 gives this manpower and skills dollar estimate for our example.

In Exhibit 6–7, the labor hours are summarized from Exhibits 6–3 through 6–6, multiplied by 400 units of each product to be produced, and totaled. Thus, from Exhibit 6–7, 720 labor hours of assembler time are estimated.

The wage rates for each skill can be obtained from the personnel department. (This should be the hourly wage rate of the employee; fringe benefits are included elsewhere in the budget.) Again as shown in Exhibit 6–7, multiplying the $5.90-per-hour rate for assemblers by the 720 hours gives an estimated total cost of assemblers of $4,248.

Laborer hours were not estimated directly by the engineering department. This laborer time could be for items like moving material, cleaning equipment, and sweeping. For the factory as a whole, laborer hours averaged 10 percent of the skills labor hours. The skills hours total 3,120, so, as a rough estimate for the first month of the new department, 312 laborer hours are estimated.

Multiplying and adding all labor categories together gives an estimated cost of $26,170 to produce all four products.

Number of employees. While the labor hours just calculated give the cost figures for your budget, you must still estimate the number of employees needed by the new department in each skill area. This involves adding to the labor hours an estimate of missed work due to items like absenteeism and vacations. This total is then divided by the number of hours per month worked to arrive at the number of people. Of course, some rounding of the results will be necessary for a practical solution.

For our Harrisonburg Company example, Exhibit 6–8 shows these calculations.

EXHIBIT 6–7

Manpower and Labor Skills Estimate

HARRISONBURG OFFICE EQUIPMENT
MANUFACTURING COMPANY
MANPOWER AND SKILLS ESTIMATING
Industrial-Engineering
Labor Estimates (Hours)—
for 400 Units of Each Product

Product

Skill	T–11	T–12	T–13	T–14
Machinist	.90	.80	1.00	.70
Laborer	.20	.20	.21	.17
Assembler	.40	.60	.40	.40
Finisher	.70	.60	.70	.60

Machinist hours = (.9) (400) + (.8) (400) + (1.0) (400) +
(.7) (400) = 1,360 hours

Laborer hours = (.2) (400) + (.2) (400) + (.21) (400) +
(.17) (400) = 312 hours

Assembler hours = (.4) (400) + (.6) (400) + (.4) (400) +
(.4) (400) = 720 hours

Finisher hours = (.7) (400) + (.6) (400) + (.7) (400) +
(.6) (400) = 1,040 hours

Total hours   = 3,432

Costs

Machinist	= 1,360 hours	× $9.60/hour	=	$13,056
Laborers	= 312	× 4.75	=	1,482
Assemblers	= 720	× 5.90	=	4,248
Finishers	= 1,040	× 7.10	=	7,384

Total Labor Costs $26,170

EXHIBIT 6–8

Number of Employees Estimate

HARRISONBURG OFFICE EQUIPMENT
MANUFACTURING COMPANY
LABOR HOURS TRANSLATED TO NUMBER OF EMPLOYEES

	Mach-inist	La-borer	Assem-bler	Fin-isher
Labor Hours	1,360	312	720	1,040
× 1.15 for allowances	× 1.15	× 1.15	× 1.15	× 1.15
= Employee hours	1,564	359	828	1,196
÷ 4⅓ weeks/month (173.2 hours)	÷ 173.2	÷ 173.2	÷ 173.2	÷ 173.2
= Number of employees	9.03	2.07	4.78	6.91
= Actual employees	9	2	5	7

Total employees = 23

In Exhibit 6–8, the required labor hours from Exhibit 6–7 are multiplied by 1.15 to arrive at the employee hours. This 15 percent addition is the companywide allowance for missed work time due to illness, absenteeism, and vacation. (This assumes these employees are not paid for hours they are absent and that vacation hours are covered under benefits in a different part of the budget.) The resultant employee hours are divided by 4⅓ weeks per month (173.2 hours) to arrive at the number of people needed per month. Thus, from Exhibit 6–8, 9.03 machinists needed would result in nine being assigned to the department, while 4.78 assemblers would result in five being assigned to the department. Thus, overall, twenty-three hourly employees should be assigned to this new department to produce 400 of each of the four new products in October.

Estimates of Material Costs

Estimating material costs involves three activities: (1) estimating the quantities of each type of material required, (2) translating these estimates into the actual costs of material required, and (3) determining the inventory status of the materials.

Quantity estimates of materials. With any luck, the industrial engineering department will already have done all the materials estimating for you. Nevertheless, you may have to do it yourself, and, in any case, understanding how the numbers are derived will help you to understand your budget. Thus, we will go through all the details of how to estimate the quantities of materials required.

From the engineering drawings of your products to be produced you can determine each specific type of material you will need. That is, you must make up a list of each different size and type material you will need and determine the length or quantity of the material that you can purchase. (You may have to check with the purchasing department to find some of this information.) From your list of materials for each component you can combine similar items and end up with a second list for purchasing and inventory control.

As an example let us consider our Harrisonburg Company example. From the engineering drawings of Exhibits 6–1 and 6–2, we can break down the computer table and printer table into individual components and determine the amount of material required for each component. These details are shown in Exhibits 6–9 through 6–14.

Exhibits 6–9 and 6–10 show the details of individual components for the metal tables while Exhibits 6–12 and 6–13 show the individual components for the wood tables. For example, the metal computer table is broken into components of legs, leg supports, top, monitor stand, and feet. Where appropriate, an allowance for the material lost in cutting (⅛″) is added to each dimension. Thus the actual

EXHIBIT 6-9

Materials Requirement, Table T-11

HARRISONBURG OFFICE EQUIPMENT MANUFACTURING COMPANY
MATERIALS REQUIREMENT, METAL COMPUTER TABLE T-11

1. Legs—1½" hollow square
   27⅞" + ⅛" cut = 28" (4 required)

2. Leg supports—1½" hollow square
   44⅞" + ⅛" cut = 45" (1 required)
   26⅞" + ⅛" cut = 27" (2 required)

3. Top—35⅞" wide × ⅛" thick
   47⅞" long + ⅛" cut = 48" (1 required)

4. Monitor stand—12" wide × ⅛" thick
   39⅞" long + ⅛" cut = 40" (1 required)

5. Feet—1 set of 4—purchased

1020 strip steel

---

leg length of 27⅞" has ⅛" added to it to indicate that a material length of 28" is required prior to cutting.

Exhibit 6-11 combines Exhibits 6-9 and 6-10 by metal dimensions, not components. Exhibit 6-14 combines Exhibits 6-12 and 6-13 by wood dimensions, not components. For example, in Exhibit 6-11, the legs and leg supports of the metal tables are made of 1½" hollow square steel. The different components are 28", 27", 33", 21", 45", and 30" long. To minimize material scrap, the first four sizes can be cut from 14' lengths and the last two sizes from 15' lengths. Taking into account the number of pieces needed for each unit, Exhibit 6-11 shows that 581 pieces of 1½" hollow square steel 14' long are necessary. To

EXHIBIT 6-10

Materials Requirement, Table T-13

HARRISONBURG OFFICE EQUIPMENT
MANUFACTURING COMPANY
MATERIALS REQUIREMENT, METAL PRINTER TABLE T-13

1. Legs—1½" hollow square
   29⅞" + ⅛" cut = 30" (4 required)

2. Leg supports—1½" hollow square
   32⅞" + ⅛" cut = 33" (1 required)
   20⅞" + ⅛" cut = 21" (2 required)

3. Top—29⅞" wide × ⅛" thick
   35⅞" long + ⅛" cut = 36" (1 required)

4. Feet—1 set of 4—purchased

5. Paper basket (wire mesh) (1 required)
   —purchased

1020 strip steel

---

this must be added an allowance for scrap and errors in machining. For the rest of the factory a 3 percent factor is normally used. Since this is your first month of operation, a 5 percent scrap allowance is felt appropriate. Thus an additional 29 14'-long pieces should be purchased and available in inventory, giving a total requirement including scrap of 610 14'-long pieces. Other metal sizes are calculated in Exhibit 6-11, and in Exhibit 6-14 for wood tables.

Estimating material costs.   Once you have the number and size of materials to be ordered, you need only multiply by the cost of each item and sum the results to determine your total estimated material costs.

100   OPERATING BUDGETS

EXHIBIT 6–11

Materials Requirement, Table T–11 and T–13

HARRISONBURG OFFICE EQUIPMENT
MANUFACTURING COMPANY
MATERIALS REQUIREMENT, BOTH METAL TABLES

---

1. 1½″ hollow square—14′ long

A. Computer table legs—28″
  6 per 14′ length   400 units × 4 per unit ÷ 6 = 267 pieces
B. Computer table leg supports—27″
  6 per 14′ length   400 units × 2 per unit ÷ 6 = 134 pieces
C. Printer leg supports—33″
  5 per 14′ length   400 units × 1 per unit ÷ 5 = 80 pieces
D. Printer leg supports—21″
  8 per 14′ length   400 units × 2 per unit ÷ 8 = 100 pieces
                 + 5% scrap allowance   29 pieces

          Total 14′-long pieces   = 610

2. 1½″ hollow square—15′ long

A. Computer table leg supports—45″
  4 per 15′ length   400 units × 1 per unit ÷ 4 = 100 pieces
B. Printer table legs—30″
  6 per 15′ length   400 units × 4 per unit ÷ 6 = 267 pieces
                 + 5% scrap allowance   19

          Total 15′-long pieces   = 386

3. 35 ⅞″ wide × ⅛″ thick—8′ long

A. Computer top—48″
  2 per 8′ length   400 units × 1 per unit ÷ 2 = 200 pieces
                 + 5% scrap allowance   10 pieces

          Total 8′-long pieces   = 210

4. 12″ wide × ⅛″ thick—10′ long

A. Computer monitor stand—40″
  3 per 10′ length   400 units × 1 per unit ÷ 3 = 134 pieces
                 + 5% scrap allowance   =   7 pieces

          Total 10′-long pieces   = 141

5. 29⅞″ wide × ⅛″ thick—12′ long

A. Printer top—36″

4 per 12′ length	400 units × 1 per unit ÷ 4	= 100 pieces
	+ 5% scrap allowance	= 5
	Total 12′-long pieces	= 105

6. Feet

800 sets + 5% scrap allowance = 840 sets

7. Paper baskets

400 baskets + 5% scrap allowance = 420 units

Details of these calculations for our Harrisonburg Office Equipment Manufacturing Company example are shown in Exhibit 6–15 for the metal tables and Exhibit 6–16 for the wood tables.

For example, in Exhibit 6–15, for the 14′, 1½″ hollow square steel material, purchasing has given you an expected price of $5.60 per piece. (Purchasing will already have taken into account any quantity discounts in giving you this figure.) Thus for material for components made from the 610 14′-long 1½″ hollow square steel, the cost is estimated to be $3,416. For all of the metal raw materials the total cost to produce 800 metal tables is $9,087, and 800 wood tables $11,789.

We are assuming that the feet and the paper basket will be purchased in finished form from suppliers and that we will not need to do any further work on them. Their costs are included in Exhibits 6–15 and 6–16 but are listed separately since they are detailed separately on the actual budget form.

Effect on inventory. The materials detailed above are needed for the month of October and hence must be

EXHIBIT 6-12

Materials Requirement, Table T-12

HARRISONBURG OFFICE EQUIPMENT
MANUFACTURING COMPANY
MATERIALS REQUIREMENT,
WOOD COMPUTER TABLE, T-12

---

1. Legs—1½" square
   27¼" long + ⅛" cut = 27⅜" (4 required)

2. Leg supports—1½" square
   44⅞" long + ⅛" cut = 45" (1 required)
   26⅞" long + ⅛" cut = 27" (2 required)

3. Top—29⅞" wide × ¾" thick
   47⅞" long + ⅛" cut = 48" (1 required)

4. Facing strip—4" wide × ¾" thick
   47⅞" long + ⅛" cut = 48" (2 required)
   29⅞" long × ⅛" cut = 30" (2 required)

5. Monitor stand—12" wide × ¾" thick
   21⅞" long + ⅛" cut = 22" (1 required)
   8⅞" long + ⅛" cut = 9" (2 required)

6. Monitor stand facing strip = 2" wide × ⅜" thick
   21⅞" long + ⅛" cut = 22" (2 required)

7. Feet—1 set of 4—purchased

---

ordered to arrive prior to October. While it's probably not your responsibility, the purchasing or scheduling departments will have to know your requirements far enough in advance so that they have time to order and receive the materials. Purchasing and scheduling should also check to see if the size materials you need are used elsewhere in the

EXHIBIT 6-13

Materials Requirement, Table T-14

HARRISONBURG OFFICE EQUIPMENT MANUFACTURING COMPANY
MATERIALS REQUIREMENT, WOOD PRINTER TABLE T-14

1. Legs—1½" square
   29¼" long + ⅛" cut = 29⅜" (4 required)

2. Leg supports—1½" square
   32⅞" long + ⅛" cut = 33" (1 required)
   20⅞" long + ⅛" cut = 21" (2 required)

3. Top—29⅞" wide × ¾" thick
   35⅞" long + ⅛" cut = 36" (1 required)

4. Facing strip—4" wide × ¾" thick
   35⅞" long + ⅛" cut = 36" (2 required)
   23⅞" long + ⅛" cut = 24" (2 required)

5. Feet—1 set of 4—purchased

6. Paper basket (wire mesh) (1 required)—purchased

---

factory so that your material needs could be combined with that of other departments. You may need to order materials well in advance of production to make sure they are on hand as needed.

Estimates of Operating Costs

Using the department's goals and objectives, the work load required, the labor costs, and the material costs, you are now ready to estimate the details of the monthly operating budget. The format for your budget is the same as that used

EXHIBIT 6-14

Materials Requirement, Tables T-12 and T-14

HARRISONBURG OFFICE EQUIPMENT
MANUFACTURING COMPANY
MATERIALS REQUIREMENT, BOTH WOOD TABLES

1. 1½″ square—14′ long

A. Computer table legs—28″
   6 per 14′ length   400 units × 4 per unit ÷ 6 = 267 pieces
B. Computer table leg supports—27″
   6 per 14′ length   400 units × 2 per unit ÷ 6 = 134 pieces
C. Printer leg supports—33″
   5 per 14′ length   400 units × 1 per unit ÷ 5 = 80 pieces
D. Printer leg supports—21″
   8 per 14′ length   400 units × 2 per unit ÷ 8 = 100 pieces
                      + 5% scrap allowance   = 29 pieces

          Total 14′-long pieces   = 610

2. 1½″ square—15′ long

A. Computer table leg supports—45″
   4 per 15′ length   400 units × 1 per unit ÷ 4 = 100 pieces
B. Printer table legs—30″
   6 per 15′ length   400 units × 4 per unit ÷ 6 = 267 pieces
                      + 5% scrap allowance   = 19

          Total 15′-long pieces   = 386

3. 29⅞″ wide × ¾″ thick—8′ long

A. Computer top—48″
   2 per 8′ length   400 units × 1 per unit ÷ 2 = 200 pieces
                     + 5% scrap allowance   = 10 pieces

          Total 8′-long pieces   = 210

4. 4″ wide × ¾″ thick—8′ long

A. Computer facing strip—48″
   2 per 8′ length   400 units × 2 per unit ÷ 2 = 400 pieces

B. Printer facing strip—24"
   4 per 8' length   400 units × 2 per unit ÷ 4 = 200 pieces
                         + 5% scrap allowance   =   30 pieces

               Total 8'- long pieces   = 630

5. 4" wide × ¾" thick—15' long

A. Computer facing strip—30"
   6 per 15' length   400 units × 2 per unit ÷ 6 = 134 pieces
B. Printer facing strip—36"
   5 per 15' length   400 units × 2 per unit ÷ 5 = 160 pieces
                         + 5% scrap allowance   =   15 pieces

               Total 15'-long pieces   = 309

6. 12" wide × ¾" thick—10' long

A. Computer monitor stand—22" + 9" + 9" = 40"
   3 per 10' length   400 units × 1 per unit ÷ 3 = 134 pieces
                         + 5% scrap allowance   =   7 pieces

               Total 10'-long pieces   = 141

7. 2" wide × ¾" thick—11' long

A. Monitor stand facing strip—22"
   6 per 11' length   400 units × 2 per unit ÷ 6 = 134 pieces
                         + 5% scrap allowance   =   7 pieces

               Total 11'-long pieces   = 141

8. 29⅞" wide × ¾" thick—12' long

A. Printer top—36"
   4 per 12' length   400 units × 1 per unit ÷ 4 = 100 pieces
                         + 5% scrap allowance   =   5 pieces

               Total 12'-long pieces   = 105

9. Feet

               800 sets + 5% scrap allowance   = 840 sets

10. Paper baskets

               400 baskets + 5% scrap allowance = 420 units

by other departments of your company as we have discussed in earlier chapters. The budget format we will use as an example contains elements common to all budgets.

For the Harrisonburg Office Equipment Manufacturing Company, Exhibit 6–17 shows a hypothetical monthly operating budget for our new computer tables department for October. Each individual cost line is numbered consistent with the example in Chapter 4. Let's look at the line item components.

1.1 Hourly labor.   Hourly labor is the variable manufacturing labor that goes directly into making the products. It is the hours and costs of labor calculated earlier.

For the Harrisonburg Company example from Exhibit 6–7 we totaled 3,432 labor hours at a total cost of $26,170. Dividing the dollars by the labor hours gives an average hourly labor cost of $7.63.

1.2 Salaried labor.   Salaried labor is the fixed cost of non-hourly employees charged directly to the new department. For our example, we assume your salary as department supervisor is the only salaried cost at the startup of the new department. Assuming you are paid $24,000 per year, October's share is $2,000.

1.3 Overtime.   Overtime is the variable-cost added amount above the normal rate paid to hourly employees for overtime in accordance with state and federal laws and company rules. In general this is 50 percent of the straight-time rate for hours over eight in a day or forty in a week. (Sometimes company rules or union agreements require double time (100 percent overtime premium) for Sunday or holiday work.) Since the regular wages are included in the hourly labor line, only the additional amount is listed here.

NEW-DEPARTMENT BUDGETING**107**

EXHIBIT 6-15

Materials Costs, Metal Tables

HARRISONBURG OFFICE EQUIPMENT
MANUFACTURING COMPANY
MATERIALS COSTS, METAL TABLES

1. 14' long—1½" hollow square
   610 pieces at $5.60   = $3,416

2. 15' long—1½" hollow square
   386 pieces at $6.00   = 2,316

3. 8' long—⅛" thick × 35⅞" wide
   210 pieces at $8.42   = 1,768

4. 10' long—⅛" thick × 12" wide
   141 pieces at $3.70   =   522

5. 12' long—⅛" thick × 29⅞" wide
   105 pieces at $10.14   = 1,065

               Total   = $9,087

6. Feet—840 sets at $.78   = $ 655

7. Paper basket—420 pieces at $1.18   =   496

          Total purchased   = $1,151

For our example, we plan no overtime in October and hence budget none.

1.4 Benefits. The salaries listed above do not include benefits such as insurance, health care, and vacation. These are listed separately to clearly identify their costs. To find out benefit costs ask the personnel or budgeting de-

EXHIBIT 6-16

Materials Costs, Wood Tables

HARRISONBURG OFFICE EQUIPMENT
MANUFACTURING COMPANY
MATERIALS COSTS, WOOD TABLES

1. 14' long—1½" square
   610 pieces at $6.10   = $3,721

2. 15' long—1½" square
   386 pieces at $6.60   =   2,548

3. 8' long—¾" thick × 29⅞" wide
   210 pieces at $9.74   =   2,045

4. 8' long—¾" thick × 4" wide
   630 pieces at $1.15   =   725

5. 15' long—¾" thick × 4" wide
   309 pieces at $2.16   =   667

6. 10' long—¾" thick × 12" wide
   141 pieces at $4.32   =   609

7. 11' long—⅜" thick × 2" wide
   141 pieces at $.80   =   113

8. 12' long—¾" thick × 29⅞" wide
   105 pieces at $12.96   =   1,361

   Total   = $11,789

9. Feet—840 sets at $.97   =   815

10. Paper basket—420 pieces at $1.18   =   496

   Total purchased   = $1,311

EXHIBIT 6-17

October Budget

HARRISONBURG OFFICE EQUIPMENT
MANUFACTURING COMPANY
COST-CENTER BUDGET
COST CENTER 22, COMPUTER TABLES DEPARTMENT
OCTOBER, 198X

Item	Unit	Quantity	Unit Cost	Total
1.1 Hourly labor	hrs	3,432	$7.63	$26,170
1.2 Salaried labor				2,000
1.3 Overtime	hrs			0
1.4 Benefits				10,346
1.5 Repair labor	hrs	140	9.93	1,390
2.1 Repair materials				200
3.1 Miscellaneous				1,000
4.1 Process supplies				5,310
5.1 Outside services				0
6.1 Utilities				810
7.1 Depreciation				6,667
8.1 Production materials:				
8.11 Wood				11,789
8.12 Metal				9,087
8.13 Other				2,462
9.1 Factory indirect cost allocation				12,012
10.1 Total				$89,243

Production: T-11 units 400
T-12 units 400
T-13 units 400
T-14 units 400

partment. They will tell you the amount to use generally expressed as a percent of all labor costs.

For our example, we found the personnel department allocated benefits at an additional 35 percent above direct salary. For this line we added hourly labor, salaried labor, and repair labor and multiplied the total by .35 to arrive at $10,346.

1.5 Repair labor. Repair labor is labor hours the maintenance department will charge for work hours done to maintain and repair your new equipment. Repair labor is normally a semi-variable cost.

For our new department example, since you have no history to go by, talk to the maintenance department and see if you can come up with a rough number to use. The maintenance department estimated that a fair amount of adjustment would be necessary for your new equipment and that 140 hours of repair labor was a reasonable estimate. This would be charged to your department at an average maintenance department cost of $9.93 an hour, for a total of $1,390.

2.1 Repair materials. Repair materials are materials the maintenance department would use in your department for equipment repair.

For our example, since there is no history, talk to the maintenance department for their estimate. We have estimated that most of the maintenance hours would be in equipment adjustment in the first month of operation and that very little material, only $200 worth, would be necessary.

3.1 Miscellaneous. Miscellaneous includes all of the small items not appropriate for other lines and not worth a separate line. This would include items like stationery supplies, instrument calibration, and travel expenses.

For our example, for the first month, we have no history as a basis for this estimate, and no real standard cost technique.

You might make a list of the miscellaneous items you anticipate, and assign a rough dollar value to them. We have assumed that this has been done, and that these items totaled $1,000.

4.1 Process supplies. Process supplies are the variable and semi-variable cost supplies directly used to produce the products. This would include items like tools for the equipment, sandpaper, and paint and finishing supplies. You must estimate each of these categories separately and add them together.

Exhibit 6–18 gives our first month's estimate for our example. The process supplies estimate is $5,310.

5.1 Outside services. Outside services would include items like a vendor's representative to fix a piece of equipment, outside maintenance work, and outside instrument calibration—that is, special charges for services performed by people outside your department that are legitimate charges to your department. For our example none were estimated for October.

6.1 Utilities. Utilities include items like heat, light, electricity, and steam. It could also include additional rented space used only by your department. If these charges can be determined separately for your department, they should be estimated and budgeted separately. Many utility charges cannot be measured separately for each department. For these cases, the utility items are allocated to each department based upon some consistent measure, such as your department's square footage compared to that of the company as a whole.

EXHIBIT 6-18

Estimated Process Supplies, October

HARRISONBURG OFFICE EQUIPMENT
MANUFACTURING COMPANY
ESTIMATED PROCESS SUPPLIES

	October
Tools and fixtures	$1,910
Varnish, lacquer, etc.*	1,680
Paint ($1.50 per metal table)	1,200
Oil, lubricants, etc.	375
Miscellaneous	145
Total	$5,310

*$.50 per metal table and $1.60 per wood table

For our example, Exhibit 6-19 shows details of utility cost calculations for October, assuming a combination of direct charges and allocated items. These estimates total $810.

7.1 Depreciation. Depreciation is the way in which the cost of your new capital equipment is written off against operating expense each month. It is the transfer of an asset to an operating expense. (More details of capitalization versus expense are provided in Chapter 9.) The amount of depreciation charged each month is an accounting decision, and you don't have any control over it. Nevertheless, it is a legitimate expense of your new department and should be listed on your budget.

EXHIBIT 6-19

Estimated Utilities, October

HARRISONBURG OFFICE EQUIPMENT MANUFACTURING COMPANY ESTIMATED UTILITIES, OCTOBER	
Heat*	$125
Electricity*†	415
Water*†	270
Steam†	0
Rental	0
Miscellaneous	0
Total	$810

†Direct meter charge to your department
*Allocated by square feet. Your new department is 30,000 square feet, 1/20 of
    the factory total.
Heat: 1/20 of $2500 = $125
Electricity: 1/20 of $6200 + $105 department metered = $415
Water: 1/20 of $3,600 + $90 department metered = $270

For our example, the accounting department said that
the total amount of new capital equipment for your new
department was $800,000 and that the accounting depart-
ment decided to depreciate it over ten years. This $80,000
per year charge then amounts to a monthly charge of $6,667.

8.11 Production materials: Wood. Production
materials would be wood used directly in producing your
products, including allowances for cutting and scrap.
    Using a rough standard-cost system, we calculated these
details in Exhibit 6-16. They totaled $11,789.

8.12 Production materials: Metal. This line item is the metal production materials used directly in producing your products, including allowances for cutting and scrap.

For our example, these details have already been calculated in Exhibit 6–15, and total $9,087.

8.13 Production materials: Other. This category includes material that goes directly into the finished product that is not a large enough dollar amount to call out as a separate line item.

For our example, this category is the feet for each table and the printer table paper baskets. From Exhibits 6–15 and 6–16 these costs total $2,462.

9.1 Factory indirect-cost allocation. Factory indirect-cost allocation is the portion of other factory expenses that go to support your department. (This is often called "overhead.") This would include items like the factory manager's salary, the security force, the shipping and receiving department, secretarial help, and the production planning department. It would not include sales department activities and accounting activities since these are generally outside the manufacturing division. You will have no control over these items but they are legitimate expenses to support your department and should be listed on your monthly budget.

Factory indirect-cost allocation can be assigned in a number of ways, such as based upon the production volume, the labor hours used, or perhaps an arbitrary dollar amount assignment.

In our example, we have followed a very common practice where factory indirect-cost allocation is charged on the basis of direct hourly labor used. The Harrisonburg Office Equipment Manufacturing Company uses $3.50 per hourly labor hour for its factory indirect-cost allocation for other departments. Thus, for our new department, 3,432 hourly labor hours were planned for October and $3.50 × 3,432, or $12,012, of factory indirect-cost allocation was estimated for October.

10.1 Total   The total is the sum of all of the different line items on the operating budget. It, of course, includes items that you can control, at least to some degree, and some items, like benefits and factory indirect-cost allocation, that you cannot control.

Nevertheless, the $89,243 total amount for our example is a reasonable judgment of the total manufacturing costs in the new department to produce 400 units of each of the four products for October.

Development of a Tentative Budget

The budget you just developed for October is a starting point. Take it to your supervisor and discuss it in detail. Go over with your supervisor the estimates of work load required, and how you arrived at the details of labor hours required. Explain to your supervisor what it means in terms of the number of employees needed and the skills needed. Also, explain to your supervisor how the future plans for work output will affect the budget. Your supervisor will have suggestions for you and may in fact change some of the considerations you used to set up your budget.

You might also want to check with the engineering, maintenance, and accounting departments about some of your estimates.

Development of a Revised Budget

With the input from your supervisor and others, revise your tentative budget to take into account their comments. This revised budget is the one you should pass on to your supervisor and the ideas incorporated in the revised budgets are the ones you should use for the future. Remember after October's work has been done, your report comparing October's actual expenses and budgeted costs gives you another input to revise future months' budgets.

QUARTERLY AND YEARLY BUDGETS

We have detailed a process for preparing an estimated budget for October. You must also repeat this process and estimate a budget for November and December. You would combine them to get an estimate of the last quarter of the year. (Details of the November, December, and quarterly budgets are provided in Chapter 8.) You can also get the sales forecasts for the next year, and estimate a rough budget for the entire year, either by starting with monthly budgets, or, as is probably more practical, starting with quarterly budgets.

Of course, nobody expects your first budget to be perfect. After October's work is performed, you will get back a report comparing October's actual expenses with your budget. This will help you identify some of the areas where your budget needs improvement. You can then revise future budgets based on this first month's experience. After a few months of comparing actual expenses with your budget, and revising the monthly budgets, you should have your budget fairly well under control. This does not mean that actual expenses will be just like your future budgets, because no one can predict the future that accurately. Nevertheless, the differences between your budget and actual expenses should decrease as you get your budget under more control.

BUDGETS, COMPUTERS, AND SPREADSHEETS

We have calculated your new department budget in a logical, consistent manner without considering whether you would actually do it by hand or on a computer. Most companies actually enter their budget on a computer, print their budget estimates by computer, update their estimates by computer, and print the actual versus budgeted cost comparison by computer. Most individuals, however, still make their budget calculations by hand, mark up an old budget printout, and return it to accounting to be updated on the computer. The increased availability of microcomputers in the last few years and the development of an accounting form called a "spreadsheet" offer a way to set up and revise budgets that can decrease the time and effort involved. In Appendix B we will give an introduction to budgeting with the aid of computers and spreadsheets.

7

MANAGEMENT
CONTROL

*"How do you use budget reports
for variance analysis
and management control?"*

MANAGEMENT CONTROL

The management-control concept, in its simplest form, says
that management must check up to see that the plans developed are actually being followed. The concept of control
thus involves measuring actual performance and comparing
the actual performance against the planned performance.
Any differences between planned and actual performance
are then noted for management to investigate. Thus, the
control concept requires a plan expressed in measurable,
quantitative terms, and a system set up to collect the data
about actual performance.

A budget is a perfect example of a quantitative, measurable management plan. In addition, every company has
an accounting system in place to collect and measure actual
dollar flow. Thus, the potential for budget control exists in
almost every company.

A management budget-control system can be set up for
all aspects of funds flow: profits, revenue, and costs. Since

we are discussing operating budgets in this section of this book, we shall concentrate on cost-management control, although you can easily see the application to profit and revenue control. In Chapter 11, we will present a comprehensive example for a non-profit organization.

THE MEANING OF VARIANCE

A budget is a plan of estimated future financial flows. In our context of operating budgets, the budget is an estimate of the costs of operating a cost center for some future time period: a month, quarter, or year. When the time period in question arrives, the costs of the actual work carried out in the department are accumulated by the accounting system (time sheets, purchase orders, material requisitions), and, at the end of the time period, these actual costs are totaled and compared to the budgeted costs. The difference between the actual cost and the budgeted cost is called the "variance" from budgeted costs.

Management must control costs if they are to make a satisfactory profit in the long run. One of management's most valuable control tools is the regular time period (monthly or quarterly) comparison of actual and budgeted costs. By analyzing these differences, the department supervisor and other management can determine why there were variances and what should be done about them in future time periods. An honest analysis of variances does not assume either that the actual costs or the budgeted costs were in error, only that the actual and budgeted costs differed. It is possible that actual costs were not well controlled. It is also possible that the budget was poorly planned and did not reasonably predict future costs. Finally, it is possible that the firm used a fixed-cost system and that actual production was higher than planned production, resulting in larger variable and semi-variable costs.

VARIANCE
MEASUREMENTS

Variances are most commonly measured in either or both of two ways: dollar amounts and percentages.

The most common variance measurement is to subtract the dollar amount of the actual cost from the dollar amount of the budget. If the budgeted amount is greater than the actual cost, the variance is considered positive. If the actual cost is greater than the budgeted amount, the variance is considered negative. (A negative variance is often placed in parentheses.) These positive or negative dollar amounts can then be analyzed as desired.

A variance expressed by a dollar amount, however, shows only part of the picture. A percentage variance allows the magnitude of the variance to be seen from a different viewpoint. The most common percentage calculation is to simply divide the dollar variance by the dollar budgeted cost. The result is the percentage variance from the budgeted amount, and is positive or negative, depending upon the sign of the dollar variance.

The most thorough variance report will compare actual and budgeted costs and detail both the dollar and the percentage variance from budget.

DEGREE OF
VARIANCE ANALYSIS

It is rare on any line item for the actual cost to be the same as the budgeted cost. After all, the budget is an estimate of an uncertain future.

The supervisor and managers at all levels must make decisions about which variances are large enough to investigate, since small variances are not worth the time and effort to investigate them.

If the variance is expressed in dollar amounts, the threshold size of the variance to be investigated must be consistent with the budgeted dollar amount. That is, if the line item is budgeted at $15,000, and the variance is a negative $200, the dollar amount is not worth the time and effort to investigate. On the other hand a $5,000 negative variance on a $15,000 budgeted line item clearly is worth investigation.

One way around this question of the size of the dollar amount to investigate is to express the variance as a percentage. Then you can set a percentage threshold, say 15 percent, and investigate all variances, positive or negative, that are more than 15 percent. While this system offers advantages over the dollar-amount variance, you can run into the line item that was budgeted at $50, actually cost $75, and hence had a percentage variance of (50 percent). Yet it is still only $25, regardless of the percentage, and is probably not worth the time to investigate.

The most practical system is to combine the two, and set a decision rule like: investigate all variances of 15 percent or larger where the actual dollar variance is $300 or larger.

Note that the figures of 15 percent and $300 were picked randomly. In general, upper-level management will set these figures at the same value for all the departments of the company. They will consider the total-cost dollar amounts involved, the financial picture of the company, and the degree of risk taking among the upper-level management, as well as other considerations. Upper-level management must resist the temptation to set these figures too low. Setting low figures may make some individuals feel they are giving cost control a high priority, when in fact they are wasting time and money in the investigation of small dollar amounts.

Upper-level management must also decide whether all variances should be investigated by the department supervisor, or only those line-item variances controllable by the department supervisor. Most companies will have the supervisor investigate all variances, even the ones not controllable by the supervisor, as a check for errors. For example, $8,000 depreciation may have been charged when only $6,000 was budgeted, for a negative variance of ($2,000), or (33 percent). This variance could be due to new capital equipment in the department just starting to be depreciated, in which case future budgets should be changed to reflect the increased depreciation. On the other hand, an error could have been made and the department could have been charged more depreciation than it should have. Only if the supervisor investigates the variance, can the reason for the variance be identified, and future corrections implemented.

VARIANCE ANALYSIS— AN EXAMPLE

Variance analysis is easier to explain using a specific example. We will use the October, 198x, budget of the computer-tables department of the Harrisonburg Office Equipment Manufacturing Company, Exhibit 6–17 in Chapter 6, as the basis for our example.

During October, the actual costs charged to the computer-tables department were accumulated by the accounting department from the time slips, purchase orders, material requisitions, and other internal paperwork. On November 15, the accounting department distributed the variance-analysis report computer printouts to all departments of the company. The variance-analysis report for the new department, cost center 22, is shown in Exhibit 7–1.

The variance-analysis report form shown in Exhibit 7–1 is a modification of the operating-budget form developed in earlier chapters. In column headings at the top of the report are listed the budgeted costs, the actual costs, and the variance, both in dollars and as a percentage of budgeted cost. Down the left side are listed the budget line items. At the bottom of the page are listed the budgeted and actual production.

The Company
Variance-Analysis Criteria

Before you as the department supervisor would begin reviewing the variance report in detail, you would have to find out what the company management desires for variance analysis. You make an appointment with your supervisor and talk over the subject.

At that meeting, your supervisor tells you that a written report is expected on all line items where the variance is over 20 percent and over $500 in either the positive or negative direction. Your supervisor further suggests that since this is the first month's results for your new department, you might want to review all the line items to aid your understanding and to aid in your planning for future budgets. As you are about to leave, your supervisor reminds you that the company uses a fixed-budget system (the most common), where the budgeted costs reflect planned production and where the budget estimates are not changed to reflect actual production.

THE VARIANCE
ANALYSIS

As you sit down with the variance-analysis report, Exhibit 7–1, for your department, you look first at the total. From line 10.1, actual costs were $96,203 compared to budgeted costs of $89,243, for a cost overrun of ($6,960) or (8 percent). Given the company criteria, and the fact that this is your first month of operation, you are quite pleased. Nevertheless, as you look at each line item, you see negative variances of up to (88 percent). Further, when you look at

EXHIBIT 7-1

Variance Analysis Report

HARRISONBURG OFFICE EQUIPMENT MANUFACTURING COMPANY
VARIANCE-ANALYSIS REPORT
COST CENTER 22, COMPUTER TABLES DEPARTMENT
OCTOBER, 198X
Date: November 15, 198X

Item	BUDGET			ACTUAL			VARIANCE			
	Quantity	Cost	Total	Quantity	Cost	Total	Quantity	Cost	Total	% Total
1.1 Hourly labor hours	3,432	$7.63	$26,170	3,645	$7.71	$28,102	(213)	($.08)	($1,932)	(7)
1.2 Salaried Labor			2,000			2,000			0	0
1.3 Overtime hours	0		0	0		0			0	0
1.4 Benefits			10,346			10,101			245	2
1.5 Repair labor hours	140	9.93	1,390	251	9.93	2,492	(111)	0	(1,102)	(79)
2.1 Repair materials			200			375			(175)	(88)

3.1	Miscellaneous	1,000	1,471	(471)	(47)
4.1	Process supplies	5,310	5,472	(162)	(3)
5.1	Outside services	0	0	0	0
6.1	Utilities	810	1,477	(667)	(82)
7.1	Depreciation	6,667	6,667	0	0
8.1	Production materials:				
8.11	Wood	11,789	10,993	796	7
8.12	Metal	9,087	11,765	(2,678)	(29)
8.13	Other	2,462	2,530	(68)	(3)
9.1	Factory indirect-cost allocation	12,012	12,758	(746)	(6)
10.1	Total	$89,243	$96,203	($6,960)	(8)
	Production: T-11 units	400	371	29	7
	T-12 units	400	380	20	5
	T-13 units	400	400	0	0
	T-14 units	400	400	0	0

EXHIBIT 7–2

Hourly-Labor Variance Analysis

Labor Category	Budgeted Hours	Actual Hours	Variance Hours	%
Machinist	1,360	1,520	(160)	(12)
Laborer	312	325	(13)	(4)
Assembler	720	678	42	6
Finisher	1,040	1,122	(82)	(8)
Total	3,432	3,645	(213)	(6)

the production figures, you are reminded that you produced fewer of the metal tables, T-11 and T-13, than you expected because of forming problems. Clearly, a line-by-line analysis is in order.

1.1 Hourly Labor

Hourly labor was 7 percent over budget. While this is not large, 213 more labor hours than were budgeted were used, for an additional cost of $1,932. Although your supervisor will not ask for this to be explained, you call accounting and ask for the detailed labor-hour figures. When you get these actual hours, you compare them with budgeted hours in a table, shown as Exhibit 7–2.

From this analysis, the only large variance was in machinist hours, which were up 160, or 12 percent. Since you had trouble machining and forming the metal tabletops, and, in fact, did not produce all the metal tables budgeted, you are not surprised that this figure is up. Otherwise, there are no surprises in your hourly-labor analysis.

1.2 Salaried Labor

Salaried labor is your salary, and was exactly what was expected.

1.3 Overtime

No overtime was budgeted and none was used, so there is no variance.

1.4 Benefits

Benefits were slightly (2 percent) smaller than expected. Since these are assigned by the personnel department, and you cannot really control them, no investigation is recommended.

1.5 Repair Labor

Repair labor was over budget by 79 percent. Specifically, 251 labor hours were used instead of the 140 budgeted. A quick call to maintenance verifies that that number of labor hours was in fact used. The maintenance supervisor reminds you of all the time put in adjusting your new equipment. The supervisor further reminds you that the 140 hours was at best a crude estimate. The maintenance supervisor also suggests that repair labor will decrease in future months. Thus, your written report to your supervisor should note that these costs were legitimate and that more equipment adjustment was needed than was expected.

2.1 Repair Materials

Repair materials were only $175 over budget. You would not need to investigate this variance formally, but you are sure it was material used by maintenance for their larger than expected number of labor hours.

3.1 Miscellaneous

Miscellaneous costs were 47 percent more than expected, but only $471. You are aware of the many small items you bought in the first month of operation and do not feel you will need as much in future months. Since you will not be asked for more detailed investigation, you do not feel a more detailed analysis is worthwhile.

4.1 Process Supplies

Process supplies were within 3 percent of budget, an excellent estimate for the first month's operations.

5.1 Outside Services

No outside services were budgeted or used.

6.1 Utilities

The actual utility cost was $667 or 82 percent over budget. A formal explanation is required. You talk to the accounting department, and they give you the breakdown on utilities for October. You summarize the details in Exhibit 7–3.

From Exhibit 7–3, heat and water were close to what was expected, but electricity was off by $642. Further, the electricity direct-metered in your department was $712, when only $105 was budgeted. You dig out and review your original budget estimates for direct-metered electricity. Boy is your face red! You find an arithmetic mistake. Recalculating, you find your direct-metered electricity estimate should have been $745. You write up your explanation ad-

EXHIBIT 7-3

Utility Variance Analysis

Utility Category	Budgeted Dollars	Actual Dollars	Variance Dollars	%
Heat	$125	$ 130	($5)	(4)
Electricity	415	1,057	(642)	(155)
Water	270	290	(20)	(7)
Steam	0	0	0	0
Rental	0	0	0	0
Miscellaneous	0	0	0	0
Total	$810	$1,477	($667)	(82)

Further: Budgeted electricity = 1/20 of $6,200 allocated, or
$310 + $105 department metered = $415

Actual electricity = $345 allocated + $712
department metered = $1,057

mitting your mistake and noting that you will revise future estimates.

7.1 Depreciation

Depreciation was as expected, so the variance is zero.

8.11 Production Materials: Wood

Wood materials were under budget by 7 percent. Since you had less scrap than expected on the wood tables, you are not surprised. In addition, one of the buyers in purchasing told you that one of the suppliers had a special lower price on one of the materials you ordered, although this price will not continue in future months.

8.12 Production Materials: Metal

The costs of metal used for the metal tables was $2,678 or 29 percent greater than budgeted. Clearly this requires a formal investigation. You again call the accounting department, and they give you the details of the material requisitions charged against your cost center. You sum them and compare the against the budgeted amount in Exhibit 7–4.

First, you find that the unit costs were higher than expected. A quick call to purchasing and you find out that your metal vendor had a 5 percent blanket price raise after your budget was made up, but before your material was ordered. Second, all metal items were used in greater quantities than expected. It appears that your overall scrap-rate estimate was low for your first month. A 9 percent figure, rather than the 5 percent used, appears more reasonable. Finally, the usage of the wider sheet stock used for the tabletops was well over budget. For one size you used 304 pieces instead of the 210 budgeted (45 percent overage); for the other size, you used 183 pieces instead of the 105 budgeted (74 percent overage).

While you knew you had trouble forming and machining the tabletops, since your actual machinist labor was greater than budgeted and since you did not produce the required number of metal tables, you were not really aware of the magnitude of the problem. While you can clearly report to your supervisor the budget overrun was due to excessive scrap material on the metal tabletops, you must also suggest ways to minimize this problem in the future. Presumably, you as department supervisor are already working on this, but you can reinforce it to your supervisor in your budget-variance analysis.

EXHIBIT 7-4

Metal-Production-Material Variance Analysis

Material	Bud-geted Price	Act-ual Price	Bud-geted Units	Act-ual Units	Vari-ance Units	%
1½″ hollow square—14′ long	$5.60	$5.88	610	659	(49)	(8)
1½″ hollow square—15′ long	6.00	6.30	386	422	(36)	(9)
35⅞″ wide × ⅛″ thick—8′ long	8.42	8.84	210	304	(94)	(45)
12″ wide × ⅛″ thick—10′ long	3.70	3.89	141	153	(12)	(9)
29⅞″ wide × ⅛″ thick—12′ long	10.14	10.65	105	183	(78)	(74)

8.13 Production Materials: Other

Other production material (the table feet and paper basket) was just about on target so no investigation is needed.

9.1 Factory Indirect-Cost Allocation

Indirect factory cost is allocated to each cost center at the rate of $3.50 per hourly labor rate. Since 213 more direct labor hours were used than expected, indirect factory cost allocation is $746 greater than budgeted.

10.1 Total

Note again that the total shows a cost overrun of $6,960 or 8 percent. While production of metal tables was a little lower than what was expected, this total dollar variance is still not bad for the first month of a new department. Note also how excessive reliance upon this total obscures the important details in the line-item budget. Clearly a line-by-line analysis is necessary.

Production

As noted in Chapter 6, the expected output was 400 units of each of the four computer tables. For the two wood tables, T-12 and T-14, this output was reached. Production of both of the metal tables fell below the desired output. Clearly, the reason was the difficulty in machining and forming the metal tabletops. The lower output of metal tables meant the fixed costs for October had to be spread over fewer units of output, raising the average unit cost.

Conclusion of Variance Analysis

Perhaps the advantages of variance analysis are obvious, but the need to give attention to the details of the line-item budget needs to be emphasized. Unless you are willing to spend the time and effort necessary to do a thorough analysis, little will be gained.

In addition to the use of the control concepts and variance analysis to explain the differences from the current budget, identification and analysis of variances serve as an input to better budget estimating in the future. In Chapter 8, we will look at revising monthly budgets.

GAMES MANAGERS PLAY

There are all sorts of games that can be played with the budget at all levels of management. From a management-control perspective, the budget can be blamed for all sorts of problems. Likewise, the budget system can be "beat" if a supervisor or manager really tries to. Nevertheless, most supervisors and managers don't try to beat the budget system but instead try to use it in the manner intended. Still, you ought to be aware of some of the games that people do try to play.

Take Action, Then Budget

Many people pride themselves on the speed with which they can take action, without worrying about a plan or budget. They make comments like "I'd rather get on with it," or "If I am successful, nobody will hold me to the budget," or "After the fact, what can they really do to me?" The attitude of these people clearly suggests that they do not consider costs to be important, or, perhaps, that other people should worry about the details, not them. This type of individual may be encouraged in a company where budget controls are loose or where upper-level management does not give the attention to budget control it should.

It's Not in the Budget

A convenient excuse for turning down new ideas or suggestions is that "It's not in the budget." This can occur at all levels of management. The budget becomes a convenient excuse for supervisors or managers who do not really want to implement a suggestion but do not want to tell an employee no. The budget is an imprecise estimate of an imperfect future. The budget can always be revised if a new idea or suggestion is really worthwhile.

The Boss Wants It

In an old joke, the colonel tells the major to start the parade at 10:00 A.M. The major tells the captain 9:45. The captain tells the lieutenant 9:30. The lieutenant tells the sergeant 9:15, and the sergeant has the soldiers ready at 8:30. Passing "the word" down the chain of command is a poor way to plan a budget. If upper-level management wants specific items included in a budget, they can modify your budget to reflect those items. Too often upper-level management doesn't really want anything, but someone in between does.

"End of the Fiscal Year" Blues

In many organizations, if you do not spend your entire budget by the end of the fiscal year, your budget for the next fiscal year is cut. Thus, if you manage your funds wisely and get your work done under budget, instead of being rewarded you will be penalized by a lower budget in the next fiscal year, regardless of the work load. In many non-profit and government organizations you will see people rush around the last few months of the fiscal year trying to spend money before they lose it. You will also see people holding up invoices until the next fiscal year or prepaying on invoices to manipulate the financial figures. Clearly, these attitudes and actions show a contempt for the budget process and sound financial management.

The Budget-Cutting Game

After your budget is prepared, someone up the line decides to cut all budgets by an arbitrary figure, say 15 percent. No consideration is given to the work that has gone into planning individual budgets or to the needs or differences among individual departments. If you anticipate this happening, you may make an honest estimate, then add 15 percent to be prepared for this arbitrary cut. Upper-level management, however, suspects you have "padded" your budget, so they cut it 25 percent. Next year you anticipate that, so you add 30 percent. The round robin continues.

While it is naive to imagine that it will ever happen, wouldn't it be nice if we didn't have to waste the time and effort on these games and could get on with serious attempts to do a better job of budgeting and financial control?

BUDGET
REVISIONS

*"How do you revise a current budget
and plan for future budgets?"*

THE CONCEPT OF
BUDGET REVISIONS

An operating budget is an estimate of the costs that will be
spent in the future. In general, we must budget for months
and even years in advance so that management can plan
profits and cash flow, and so that the company can be prepared for new capital investments. The further in advance
we must budget, the less accurate the budget is likely to
be. Thus, as the time for which we budgeted approaches,
we can improve the accuracy of the budget if we update it
with the latest information we have. In concept, a budget
revision requires a review of the assumptions under which
the budget was planned to determine if any of the assumptions have changed. If the assumptions have changed, a
revision is necessary.

In addition, even if the assumptions are correct, the
actual past history may show that the cost data derived from
the assumptions need to be changed. That is, a variance

analysis of past budgets may give specific clues as to where the actual costs differed from the budgeted costs.

In this chapter we will look at budget revisions in two parts. The first takes the October budget for the computer tables department and revises it into a budget for November and December. Again, these budgets would be developed in advance of any production. In the second part, we will assume that we need to revise December's budget based upon a change in production quantity from the original budget, and based upon the results of the variance analysis of the first actual month of operation, October.

If you have a microcomputer available, or if your company has terminals that let you sign on the main computer, you may be able to revise budgets with less manual work using special computer programs the company has developed, perhaps in a spreadsheet format. Our work in the balance of this chapter assumes a handwritten process, but you can easily see how you could carry it out on the computer if one is available.

COMPUTER TABLES DEPARTMENT—NOVEMBER AND DECEMBER BUDGETS

In Chapter 6 we developed a budget for the first month, October, of the new computer tables department of our Harrisonburg Company. This budget was shown in Exhibit 6–17. At the same time, we also would have developed budgets for November and December, and combined these for a quarterly budget. The starting point for the November and December budgets would be the October budget, so we could say the November and December budgets are revisions of the October budget. Exhibits 8–1 and 8–2 are the November and December budgets derived from the October

EXHIBIT 8-1

NOVEMBER Budget

HARRISONBURG OFFICE EQUIPMENT
MANUFACTURING COMPANY
COST-CENTER BUDGET
COST CENTER 22, COMPUTER-TABLES DEPARTMENT
NOVEMBER, 198X

Item		Unit	Quantity	Cost	Total
1.1	Hourly labor	hours	4,288	$7.63	$32,716
1.2	Salaried labor				2,000
1.3	Overtime	hours			0
1.4	Benefits				12,498
1.5	Repair labor	hours	100	9.93	993
2.1	Repair materials				200
3.1	Miscellaneous				800
4.1	Process supplies				5,680
5.1	Outside services				0
6.1	Utilities				1,055
7.1	Depreciation				6,667
8.1	Production materials:				
8.11	Wood				14,715
8.12	Metal				11,340
8.13	Other				3,077
9.1	Factory indirect-cost allocation				15,008
10.1	Total				$106,749

Production: T-11 units 500
             T-12 units 500
             T-13 units 500
             T-14 units 500

EXHIBIT 8-2

December Budget

HARRISONBURG OFFICE EQUIPMENT
MANUFACTURING COMPANY
COST-CENTER BUDGET
COST CENTER 22, COMPUTER-TABLES DEPARTMENT
DECEMBER, 198X

Item		Unit	Quantity	Cost	Total
1.1	Hourly labor	hours	5,145	$7.63	$39,258
1.2	Salaried labor				2,000
1.3	Overtime	hours			0
1.4	Benefits				14,788
1.5	Repair labor	hours	100	9.93	993
2.1	Repair materials				200
3.1	Miscellaneous				700
4.1	Process supplies				6,240
5.1	Outside services				0
6.1	Utilities				1,195
7.1	Depreciation				6,667
8.1	Production materials:				
8.11	Wood				17,658
8.12	Metal				13,608
8.13	Other				3,692
9.1	Factory indirect-cost allocation				18,008
10.1	Total				$125,007

Production: T-11 units 600
T-12 units 600
T-13 units 600
T-14 units 600

budget prior to October. Let us look at how these budgets would have been developed.

The starting point of our October budget was the quantity of production required. Four hundred units of each of our four tables, T-11, T-12, T-13, and T-14, were desired for October. This was a work load of 50 percent of the capacity of the department's equipment. For November, the production-planning department asked you to budget to produce 500 of each of the four tables, and to budget to produce 600 of each of the four tables in December. Let us look in detail at how we would do these budget revisions by line item.

1.1 Hourly Labor

Hourly labor is a clear-cut example of a variable cost. That is, hourly labor should go up or down in direct relationship to output. In Chapter 6, we noted that the industrial-engineering department would have established standard labor-hour data for producing our four tables. These data were presented in Exhibits 6–3 through 6–6 and summarized in Exhibit 6–7. Thus, from Exhibit 6–7, 0.9 hours of machinist time (including allowances) were estimated to be required on table T-11. In Exhibit 6–7, we then totaled labor hours for all the production by labor skills and multiplied by hourly wage rates to come up with the dollar budget estimates. This technique is fine for one month's budget but is awkward to use for budget revisions. For budget revisions, an average hourly labor cost per unit would be more useful. The total cost data from Exhibit 6–7 are translated into unit costs in Exhibit 8–3.

In Exhibit 8–3, the labor hours for each table in each of the four labor categories are multiplied by the hourly wage rate. These dollar estimates for each labor category are then added together to give a total hourly labor cost for each product. Thus, for metal computer table T-11, 0.9

EXHIBIT 8–3

Estimated Hourly Labor, November and December

HARRISONBURG OFFICE EQUIPMENT
MANUFACTURING COMPANY
ESTIMATED HOURLY LABOR, NOVEMBER AND DECEMBER

Skill	T-11	T-12	T-13	T-14
Machinist	$.9 \times 9.60 = 8.64$	$.8 \times 9.60 = 7.68$	$1.0 \times 9.60 = 9.60$	$.7 \times 9.60 = 6.72$
Laborer	$.2 \times 4.75 = .95$	$.2 \times 4.75 = .95$	$.21 \times 4.75 = 1.00$	$.17 \times 4.75 = .81$
Assembler	$.4 \times 5.90 = 2.36$	$.6 \times 5.90 = 3.54$	$.4 \times 5.90 = 2.36$	$.4 \times 5.90 = 2.36$
Finisher	$.7 \times 7.10 = 4.97$	$.6 \times 7.10 = 4.26$	$.7 \times 7.10 = 4.97$	$.6 \times 7.10 = 4.26$
Total	$16.92	$16.43	$17.93	$14.15

Hourly labor: November = (16.92) (500) + (16.43) (500) + (17.93) (500) + (14.15) (500) = $32,716

December = (16.92) (600) + (16.43) (600) + (17.93) (600) + (14.15) (600) = $39,258 hours of machinist time are multiplied by a $9.60 hourly rate to give a machinist cost of $8.64 for each unit of T-11. Assembler hours of 0.4 are multiplied by an hourly rate of $5.90 to give an assembler cost of $2.36 for each unit of T-11 produced. Adding together the four labor categories gives an estimated cost for hourly labor of $16.92 to produce one unit of T-11. In the same way, T-12 costs $16.43, T-13 $17.93, and T-14 $14.15.

For November, 500 units of each table are desired, so multiplying each unit cost by 500 and summing give a total expected hourly labor cost of $32,716. This value is then placed on line 1.1. In a similar manner, the total hours could be calculated to arrive at 4,288 labor hours. Dividing 4,288 into $32,716 gives an expected average labor cost per hour of $7.63.

For December, 600 units of each table are desired, so the same costs per unit are multiplied by 600 and summed. As shown in Exhibit 8-3, this total is $39,258, which is placed on line 1.1 of the December budget in Exhibit 8-2.

1.2 Salaried Labor

Your $2,000 monthly salary as department supervisor was charged in October. This is a fixed cost that does not change with output at these levels, so $2,000 should also be budgeted in November and December.

1.3 Overtime

Since your department is operating below capacity and the customer demand for your tables is not established, no overtime is planned for any of the three months. If desired production is not reached in any month, a decision can be reached at that time as to whether overtime should be used.

1.4 Benefits

Benefits are allocated as a variable cost at 35 percent of the total of hourly labor, salaried labor, and repair labor dollars. For November, these labor dollars totaled $35,709. Multiplying $35,709 by .35 gives an estimate of benefits of $12,498. For December, the labor costs totaled $42,251, so $14,788 was estimated for benefits.

1.5 Repair Labor

Repair labor, a semi-variable cost, was estimated at 140 hours for October but should drop off in November and December as the new equipment is broken in. One hundred hours were estimated by the maintenance department for both November and December. The maintenance average labor rate is $9.93 an hour, so $993 was budgeted in both November and December.

2.1 Repair Materials

With new equipment, the only repair material needed should be miscellaneous material to support the maintenance personnel. Two hundred dollars was estimated by the maintenance department for each of the three months. Repair material is a semi-variable cost that varies more with maintenance work than with production output.

3.1 Miscellaneous

Miscellaneous is the budget line for items too small to be detailed on a separate line. For October, the first month of operation of the new department, $1,000 was estimated. After October, you determined that some of the start-up

EXHIBIT 8–4

Estimated Process Supplies, November and December

HARRISONBURG OFFICE EQUIPMENT
MANUFACTURING COMPANY
ESTIMATED PROCESS SUPPLIES

	November	December
Tools and fixtures	$1,510	$1,300
Varnish, lacquer, etc.*	2,100	2,520
Paint ($1.50 per metal table)	1,500	1,800
Oil, lubricants, etc.	425	475
Miscellaneous	145	145
Total	$5,680	$6,240

*$.50 per metal table and $1.60 per wood table

miscellaneous costs would not be necessary in future months, so $800 was budgeted for November, and $700 for December. Miscellaneous costs vary per month, but not necessarily in proportion to output.

4.1 Process Supplies

Some process supplies vary with output, while others do not. Exhibit 6–18 shows the process supplies estimates for October, and Exhibit 8–4 estimates these values for November and December.

From Exhibit 8–4, tools and fixtures are assumed to go down from October's $1,910 estimate to $1,510 in November and $1,300 in December. The assumption is that there were some start-up costs in October, and that tooling costs should settle down to a more consistent figure after a few months. Thirteen hundred dollars was the amount of tools and fixtures per month estimated necessary after the department settled down based upon the experience of other departments in the factory. Varnish, paint, and lubricants are assumed to vary roughly in proportion to output, while a fixed miscellaneous cost is estimated each month. Totaling the individual processing supplies categories in Exhibit 8–4 gives a November estimate of $5,680 and a December estimate of $6,240.

5.1 Outside Services

No outside services were anticipated in any of the three months, so no costs were budgeted.

6.1 Utilities

October's utilities were estimated in Exhibit 7–19, and these data were revised in Exhibit 8–5 for November and December.

Heat is allocated to your department based upon your space relative to the factory as a whole. Electricity and water each have two different variable cost components. Some utility usage is metered in the department and charged directly to the department. Other utility usage is charged to the entire factory and allocated to the department based upon square footage. For example, for November, water for the factory is estimated at $3,600, based upon past usage, and you are allocated $\frac{1}{20}$ or $180, of it. In addition, you have checked with other departments with operations like yours. Based upon their experience, you estimate that you will use an additional $110 of water directly metered in your department. This gives a total estimated water utility cost of $290 for November.

EXHIBIT 8-5

Estimated Utilities, November and December

HARRISONBURG OFFICE EQUIPMENT
MANUFACTURING COMPANY
ESTIMATED UTILITIES

	November	**December**
Heat*	$310	$390
Electricity*†	455	495
Water*†	290	310
Steam†	0	0
Rental	0	0
Miscellaneous	0	0
Total	$1,055	$1,195

---

†Direct meter charge to your department
*Allocated by square feet. Your new department is 30,000 square feet, ¹⁄₂₀ of the factory total.
Heat: ¹⁄₂₀ of ($6,200, Nov.) ($7,800, Dec.) = ($310, Nov.) ($390, Dec.)
Electricity: ¹⁄₂₀ of $6,200 + ($145, Nov.) ($185, Dec.) department metered = ($455, Nov.) ($495, Dec.)
Water: ¹⁄₂₀ of $3,600 + ($110, Nov.) ($130, Dec.) department metered = ($290, Nov.) ($310, Dec.)

By adding up the individual utility costs, $1,055 is budgeted for November and $1,195 for December.

7.1 Depreciation

Depreciation is based upon the dollar value of the equipment and is a fixed cost not related to output. Thus, for all three months, the same depreciation, $6,667, was budgeted.

8.11 Production Materials: Wood

Production materials costs are costs that vary directly with output. From the engineering drawings of the four tables in Chapter 6, Exhibits 6–9 through 6–16 broke down the tables into individual parts, combined the parts into raw-material size categories, determined the optimum dimensions of raw materials to purchase, added a reasonable scrap percentage, and multiplied by the purchasing cost to determine the cost of raw materials.

While this was a reasonable approach for October's budget, a unit-cost approach is more appropriate for estimating and revising future months' budgets. Exhibit 8–6 details the unit material-cost calculations for the wood tables, T-12 and T-14.

Exhibit 8–6 restates the data of Exhibits 6–12, 6–13, 6–14, and 6–16 on a unit-cost basis. Each individual component of material needed is listed. The larger pieces of wood from which each individual component is cut are also noted. The cost per unit of each component is calculated, and the cost of all components are added together to get a total unit material cost.

As an example, consider item 1 of Table T-12 in Exhibit 8–6. Item 1 is the table legs. Four legs made of 1½″-square wood 27⅜″ long are necessary. (This length includes an allowance for cutting the leg from a longer length of wood.) In the calculations in Chapter 6 it was found that a standard length for this 1½″-square wood was 14′, that six legs could be cut from a 14′ length, and that the 14′ length cost $6.10. Since the table needs four legs, ⁴⁄₆ or ⅔ of a 14′ length is used for one table. In terms of costs, ⁴⁄₆ of $6.10, or $4.07, is the cost of the four legs for one unit (table) of output. The costs of all eight of the components are figured in a similar way, and added together to give a cost of $16.20 for material costs for Table T-12. To this figure is added a 5 percent allowance for scrap (higher

EXHIBIT 8–6

Estimated Material Costs per Unit, Wood Tables

**HARRISONBURG OFFICE EQUIPMENT
MANUFACTURING COMPANY
ESTIMATED MATERIALS COSTS PER UNIT, WOOD TABLES**

TABLE T–12

---

1. Legs—1½″ square × 27⅞″ (4 required)
   6 per 14′ at $6.10   4/6 × 6.10   = $4.07

2. Leg supports—1½″ square × 45″
   (1 required)
   4 per 15′ at $6.60   ¼ × 6.60   =   1.65

3. Leg supports—1½″ square × 27″
   (2 required)
   6 per 14′ at $6.10   ⅓ × 6.10   =   2.03

4. Top—29⅞″ × ¾″ × 48″ (1 required)
   2 per 8′ at $9.74   ½ × 9.74   =   4.87

5. Facing strip—4″ × ¾″ × 48″ (2 required)
   2 per 8′ at $1.15   ²⁄₂ × 1.15   =   1.15

6. Facing strip—4″ × ¾″ × 30″ (2 required)
   6 per 15′ at $2.16   ⅓ × 2.16   =   .72

7. Monitor stand—12″ × ¾″ × 22″
   (1 required)
   12″ × ¾″ × 9″
   (2 required)
   3 sets per 10′ at $4.32   ⅓ × 4.32   =   1.44

8. Monitor stand facing strip—2″ × ⅜″ × 22″
   (2 required) 6 per 11′ at $.80   ⅓ × .80 =   .27

   Sub-total   =   16.20
   + 5% scrap   =   .81

   Total   = $17.01

TABLE T–14

1. Legs—1½″ square × 29⅜″ (4 required)			
6 per 15′ at $6.60	4/6 × 6.60	=	$4.40
2. Leg supports—1½″ square × 33″ (1 required)			
5 per 14′ at $6.10	1/5 × 6.10	=	1.22
3. Leg supports—1½″ square × 21″ (2 required)			
8 per 14′ at $6.10	2/8 × 6.10	=	1.53
4. Top—29⅞″ × ¾″ × 36″ (1 required)			
4 per 12′ at $12.96	¼ × 12.96	=	3.24
5. Facing strip—4″ × ¾″ × 36″ (2 required)			
5 per 15′ at $2.16	2/5 × 2.16	=	.86
6. Facing strip—4″ × ¾″ × 24″ (2 required)			
4 per 8′ at $1.15	2/4 × 1.15	=	.58
Sub-total		=	11.83
+ 5% scrap		=	.59
Total		=	$12.42

than the 3 percent allowed in the rest of the factory, but reasonable for a new department in the first few months), giving a total material cost for table T-12 of $17.01.

In a similar manner, the total material cost for table T-14 is calculated at $12.42 (including scrap) in Exhibit 8–6.

For November, the total wood production material costs can then be estimated by multiplying 500 units planned production of T-12 by its cost of $17.01 and 500 units planned of T-14 by its cost of $12.42 and adding them together. In a formula: (500)(17.01) + (500)(12.42) =

$14,715. For December, $(600)(17.01) + (600)(12.42) =$ $17,658.

8.12 Production Materials: Metal

Metal production materials are also costs that vary directly with output. Exhibit 8–7 calculates on a unit-cost basis the material component and cost data for the metal tables from Exhibits 6–9, 6–10, 6–11 and 6–16.

As with the wood tables, Exhibit 8–7 lists each metal component, identifies the length of metal it will be cut from, calculates the unit cost of the component, adds a scrap estimate, and calculates a total cost of $13.17 per unit of table T-11 and $9.51 per unit of table T-13.

Total metal costs for the budget are then found by multiplying planned production by these unit costs. For November, $(500)(13.17) + (500)(9.51) = $11,340$. For December, $(600)(13.17) + (600)(9.51) = $13,608$.

8.13 Production Materials: Other

Other production materials are the feet for the tables and the paper baskets for the printer tables purchased from outside vendors. They are a cost that varies directly with output. From Exhibits 6–15 and 6–16, feet for the metal tables cost $.78 a set of four, feet for the wood tables cost $.97 a set of four, and the paper baskets cost $1.18 each. (The same paper basket is used on both the metal and the wood printer table.) A 5 percent scrap allowance is allowed for damage in the factory.

For November, 1,050 sets of metal feet are purchased ($819), 1,050 sets of wood feet are purchased ($1,019), and 1,050 paper baskets are purchased ($1,239), for a total purchased cost of $3,077.

For December, 1,260 sets of metal feet are purchased ($983), 1,260 sets of wood feet are purchased ($1,222), and 1,260 paper baskets are purchased ($1,487), for a total purchased cost of $3,692.

EXHIBIT 8-7

Estimated Material Costs per Unit, Metal Tables

HARRISONBURG OFFICE EQUIPMENT
MANUFACTURING COMPANY
ESTIMATED MATERIALS COSTS PER UNIT, METAL TABLES

TABLE T-11

1. Legs—1½" hollow square × 28" (4 required)
   6 per 14' at $5.60   ⁴⁄₆ × 5.60   = $3.73

2. Leg supports—1½" hollow square × 45"
   (1 required) 4 per 15' at $6.00   ¼ × 6.00   =   1.50

3. Leg supports—1½" hollow square × 27"
   (2 required) 6 per 14' at $5.60   ²⁄₆ × 5.60 =   1.87

4. Top—35⅞" × ⅛" × 48" (1 required)
   2 per 8' at $8.42   ½ × 8.42   =   4.21

5. Monitor stand—12" × ⅛" × 40" (1 required)
   3 per 10' at $3.70   ⅓ × 3.70   =   1.23

   Sub-total   = 12.54
   + 5% scrap   =   .63

   Total   = $13.17

TABLE T-13

1. Legs—1½" hollow square × 30" (4 required)
   6 per 15' at $6.00   ⁴⁄₆ × 6.00   = $4.00

2. Leg supports—1½" hollow square × 33"
   (1 required) 5 per 14' at $5.60   ⅕ × 5.60   =   1.12

3. Leg supports—1½" hollow square × 21"
   (2 required) 8 per 14' at $5.60   ²⁄₈ × 5.60 =   1.40

4. Top—29⅞" × ⅛" × 36" (1 required)
   4 per 12' at $10.14   ¼ × 10.14   =   2.54

   Sub-total   =   9.06
   + 5% scrap   =   .45

   Total   = $9.51

9.1 Factory Indirect-Cost Allocation

Factory indirect-cost allocation is the variable cost allocated to this department to help cover the costs of indirect expenses like managers' salaries and factory security that benefit this department but are not charged directly to the department. Our company allocates this charge to each department at the rate of $3.50 for each hourly labor hour budgeted. Thus, for November, 4,288 hourly labor hours times $3.50 is $15,008. For December, 5,145 times $3.50 is $18,008.

10.1 Total

Summing the above line items gives a total of $106,749 for November, and $125,007 for December.

THE FOURTH-QUARTER BUDGET— COMPUTER TABLES DEPARTMENT

The budget for the fourth quarter of the year is then easily calculated by adding together the monthly budgets for October, November, and December. This is shown in Exhibit 8–8.

Thus, for the fourth quarter, a total departmental budget of $320,999 is estimated.

If desired, future months' budgets could be calculated in a similar way, and a yearly budget totaled from the monthly or quarterly budgets.

REVISING DECEMBER'S BUDGET

During the month of October, as work was progressing, actual costs were accumulated. After October was over, a

EXHIBIT 8-8

Fourth-Quarter Budget

HARRISONBURG OFFICE EQUIPMENT
MANUFACTURING COMPANY
COST-CENTER BUDGET
COST CENTER 22, COMPUTER-TABLES DEPARTMENT
Fourth Quarter, 198X

Item		Unit	Quantity	Cost	Total
1.1	Hourly labor	hours	12,865	$7.63	$98,144
1.2	Salaried labor				6,000
1.3	Overtime	hours			0
1.4	Benefits				37,632
1.5	Repair labor	hours	340	9.93	3,376
2.1	Repair materials				600
3.1	Miscellaneous				2,500
4.1	Process supplies				17,230
5.1	Outside services				0
6.1	Utilities				3,060
7.1	Depreciation				20,001
8.1	Production materials:				
8.11	Wood				44,162
8.12	Metal				34,035
8.13	Other				9,231
9.1	Factory indirect-cost allocation				45,028
10.1	Total				$320,999

Production: T-11 units 1,500
T-12 units 1,500
T-13 units 1,500
T-14 units 1,500

variance-analysis report was issued comparing October's budgeted and actual costs and identifying the differences. This variance report was discussed in Chapter 7. Unfortunately, however, the variance report was not issued until November 15. By the time the supervisor had analyzed the variances and reported to upper-level management it was November 20. A revision of November's budget would have little meaning since November was almost over. At about the same time, the production-planning department called the computer-tables department supervisor and asked the supervisor to cut back the planned production for December of metal computer tables to 550 each from the planned 600 units each. (It appears that, from the short sales history, the metal tables were not selling as well as the wood tables.)

Given the timing, the supervisor should revise the budget for December to take into account both the cut in production and any changes identified from the variance analysis of October. The revised budget is shown in Exhibit 8–9. Let us look at a line-item revision of the December budget in detail.

The revision (dated November 25) in Exhibit 8–9 is an update of Exhibit 8–2, the original December budget. Remember that the company rule for explaining and correcting budget variances is a dollar amount over $500 and a percentage over 20 percent in either direction.

1.1 Hourly Labor

The October variance analysis showed costs exceeded budget by 7 percent so no revision is necessary from October's results. Since hourly labor is a variable cost, however, it should be changed to reflect the decreased production. Using the unit-cost data developed in Exhibit 8–3, and multiplying by the planned production we get the formula: ($16.92)(550 units of T-11) + ($16.43)(600 units of T-12) + ($17.93)(550 units of T-13) + ($14.15)(600 units of T-14) = $37,516.

EXHIBIT 8-9

Revised December Budget

HARRISONBURG OFFICE EQUIPMENT
MANUFACTURING COMPANY
COST-CENTER BUDGET
COST CENTER 22, COMPUTER-TABLES DEPARTMENT
(Revised: November 25, 198X)
DECEMBER, 198X

Item		Unit	Quantity	Cost	Total
1.1	Hourly labor	hours	4,923	$7.62	$37,516
1.2	Salaried labor				2,000
1.3	Overtime	hours			0
1.4	Benefits				14,178
1.5	Repair labor	hours	100	9.93	993
2.1	Repair materials				200
3.1	Miscellaneous				700
4.1	Process supplies				6,040
5.1	Outside services				0
6.1	Utilities				1,865
7.1	Depreciation				6,667
8.1	Production materials:				
8.11	Wood				17,658
8.12	Metal				13,096
8.13	Other				3,548
9.1	Factory indirect-cost allocation				17,231
10.1	Total				$121,692

Production: T-11 units 550
T-12 units 600
T-13 units 550
T-14 units 600

This dollar amount is entered on line 1.1. In a similar way, the labor hours of the four labor categories on the four tables are combined to give a total of 4,923 labor hours. Dividing labor hours into the total dollar amount gives an average cost per labor hour of $7.62.

1.2 Salaried Labor

Salaried labor remains at $2,000 since the October variance was zero, and no change is contemplated.

1.3 Overtime

The overtime variance was zero. Since no overtime is planned, the dollar amount remains at zero.

1.4 Benefits

Benefits showed a 2 percent variance for October of budget over actual costs. Benefits, however, are a variable cost based upon labor hours. Since the hourly labor has changed, the benefit budget must change. Totaling $37,516 hourly labor, $2,000 salaried labor, and $993 repair labor gives a total labor of $40,509. Since benefits are estimated at 35 percent of labor costs, the revised benefit estimate is therefore $14,178.

1.5 Repair Labor

For October, repair labor was overspent by 79 percent. An investigation found that this was extra adjustment on your new equipment. Neither you nor the maintenance department expect it to be this high in future months. So, you decide to leave repair labor at the $993 amount estimated in your first December budget.

2.1 Repair Materials

For October, repair materials were 88 percent over budget. This was only a small amount, $175, so no investigation was carried out. You feel it was due to the extra maintenance adjustment in October and that no December budget revision is necessary. Hence, you leave the original $200 estimate.

3.1 Miscellaneous

While miscellaneous supplies were over the October budget, the dollar amount was not large. You feel you have no information on which to base a change in your original $700 December estimate.

4.1 Process Supplies

Process supplies were very close to budget in October. Nevertheless, part of the process supplies are variable costs and should be revised with change in output. For a decrease in 100 metal tables you save $1.50 per table on paint, and $.50 per table on varnish, for a total of $200. Process supplies then drop to an estimated amount of $6,040. (You could make a strong argument that a $200 revision is not worth the time and effort; we included it here to emphasize that all variable costs change with output, even if you choose not to change the budget.

5.1 Outside Services

No outside services were used in October, and none are planned in December, so the amount remains at zero.

6.1 Utilities

Utilities were off in October by 82 percent because of an error in arithmetic. You budgeted $105 for direct-metered electricity instead of $745, and the $745 figure would have made your electricity variance very small. Your December direct-metered electricity budget in Exhibit 8–5 was $185 when, with your corrected calculations, it should have been $855. Thus, you underestimated direct-metered electricity by $670. Adding $670 to your original December utility estimate gives a new estimate of $1,865.

7.1 Depreciation

Depreciation is a fixed cost that does not vary with output and remains at $6,667.

8.11 Production Materials: Wood

In October, wood production-materials usage was very close to budget, and no production output change is planned for December. Thus, the original December estimate of $17,658 should continue to be used.

8.12 Production Materials: Metal

In October, the cost of metal used exceeded the budget by 29 percent. Your investigation attributed this to two causes. The first was an across-the-board price increase of 5 percent. The second was too much scrap, particularly on the table-tops. You feel the scrap problem is now under control, but you will need to adjust the December budget upward for the 5 percent price increase. On the other hand, you will need to adjust the December budget downward to reflect the production output cut in metal tables. For table T-11 the unit cost of $12.54 increased by 5 percent is $13.17; adding 5 percent scrap gives a new unit total cost of $13.82. For Table T-13, the unit cost of $9.06 increased by 5 percent is $9.51; adding 5 percent scrap gives a new unit total metal-materials cost of $9.99. Total metal costs then become:

($13.82)(550 units) + ($9.99)(550 units) = $13,096. Thus, after taking into account both the price increase and the production decrease the new estimate is $13,096 compared to the original estimate of $13,608.

8.13 Production Materials: Others

Other production materials include the table feet and printer paper baskets, purchased from outside vendors. With a 5 percent scrap allowance, you now need 1,155 (1,100 × 1.05) sets of metal feet, 1,260 (1,200 × 1.05) sets of wood feet, and 1,208 (1,150 × 1.05) paper baskets. Multiplying by the unit costs and adding, you get: (1,155)($.78) + (1,260)($.97) + (1,208)($1.18) = $3,548. This new cost of other materials replaces the original estimate on line 8.13.

9.1 Factory Indirect-Cost Allocation

Factory indirect-cost allocation is a variable cost based upon the number of hourly labor hours budgeted. Since the hourly labor hours have decreased from 5,145 to 4,923, at a $3.50 per hour rate, the factory indirect-cost allocation budget decreases to $17,231.

10.1 Total

With all these changes, the total budget for December has decreased from $125,007 to $121,692.

BUDGET REVISIONS REVISITED

As is clear from this chapter, a great deal of work is necessary to develop a budget from past budgets and to revise a monthly budget based upon new information from variance analyses and upon changes in the production output. It is imperative that your budgets be revised line by line, since major problems can be hidden in the summary numbers if you do not look at the details. Budget revisions are not easy, but they must be undertaken if financial planning and management control are to be useful to the company. The use of computers and spreadsheets can minimize the time necessary in budget revisions.

PART III

OTHER TOPICS IN BUDGETING

9

CAPITAL
BUDGETING

*"What is capital budgeting
and how do you use it?"*

CAPITAL INVESTMENT
IN THE COMPANY

Capital investment involves spending money for assets that will benefit the corporation over a number of years in the future. Capital assets include items like factory equipment, computers, typewriters, automobiles, store fixtures, and office furniture. Capital assets are assets to the firm which involve the investment of large amounts of money and which are used more than one year. The actual dollar amounts and number of years required to place an asset into the capital investment category will vary from company to company. A company might, for example, define capital equipment as equipment which costs more than $1,000 and will be in use for more than three years.

The decision-making process for capital investment is a critical one to the long-term life of a company due to the large amounts of money involved, the uncertainty in predicting future market needs, and the difficulty in gathering realistic long-term cost, revenue, and profit estimates. Because these assets will be used in an uncertain future, many things can go wrong. The equipment purchased might become obsolete sooner than expected. The market for the product the equipment was purchased to produce may not materialize. A new building may not be needed. Expected savings may not occur. The decision-making process for capital investment must take into account these risks in addition to the more normal problems associated with future estimates in the cost-accounting system.

NEED FOR
CAPITAL BUDGETING

In order to gather data for the decision-making process and for the evaluation of completed capital projects, management needs a capital budgeting system as part of its cost-accounting system. Procedures and policies for initiating capital expenditure requests, gathering of costs and benefits data, review, and evaluation of proposed capital expenditures provide a base for managerial decision-making for selecting capital equipment projects to be funded. Supervisors and managers at every level should understand the capital budgeting system and its role in the decision-making process within the company, if the company is to make the best use of its capital investment dollars.

As a supervisor or manager, you may be asked to develop and justify capital equipment budgets for your department. For example, machines in your department may need to be replaced. As a member of the management team, you may have excellent ideas for increasing productivity, raising employees' morale, or improving product quality which should be brought to the attention of upper-level management. In addition, you must be able to recognize capital expenditures when they occur, if your budgets are to be prepared accurately. When capital-expenditure proposals are being prepared or reviewed by management, you may be asked to supply cost figures or other information needed in the proposal evaluation. You may also be asked to supervise the implementation of a capital project. Finally, as a supervisor you need to be aware of capital projects which will have future impact on your area. As a result, you should understand some capital-budgeting concepts if you are to be effective in developing budgets.

CAPITALIZATION VERSUS EXPENSE

In theory, items which benefit the company over a number of years in the future should be treated as a capital-budget item with costs written off as depreciation over a specified number of years. Items that offer short-run benefits should be treated as a normal cost of doing business and charged as an expense on the current years' profit-and-loss statement. In practice, however, the decision on what items to expense and what to capitalize may be difficult. To complicate matters further, the Internal Revenue Service sets rules on capitalization and expense for companies.

Your company will have established a company policy for determining whether items should be capitalized or expensed in the current year. You must know company policy in order to prepare your budgets. You must be able to identify capital-equipment items under company policy so that you can follow capital-budgeting procedures.

A general rule of thumb may be useful in determining whether an item should be treated as a capital-budget item or an expense. A capital-budget item might include any money paid out for land, new buildings and equipment, or permanent improvements or betterments made to increase the value of either new or existing property. On the other hand, an expense might include money spent to maintain or restore existing property to its original operating efficiency and life.

The following are examples of possible capital expenditures:

1. Land acquisitions and permanent improvements to land.

2. New buildings, equipment, and processes or systems.

3. Improvements to property (buildings and/or equipment) which either:

    a. substantially increase the value of an asset as measured by capacity, speed, quality, or safety.

    b. make the asset substantially more efficient or give it new or additional functions, or

    c. substantially prolong the useful life of the property.

Generally, some minimum monetary standard (say $1,000) will be applied in evaluating items for capitalization. When you are in doubt, ask your supervisor or engineering department.

Examples of items which would normally be expensed are:

1. Minor replacements of parts or components with identical or near-identical materials or which merely restore the property

2. Repainting a building or area

3. Routine repair of machinery or other equipment

Overall, the decision as to what is capital and what is expense is an engineering and accounting one. Consequently, the engineering department is generally responsible for determining what is capital and what is expense. The engineering department should, of course, check closely with the accounting department since the accounting people must perform the actual calculations, and since accounting definitions can play an important part in the final decisions.

TYPES OF CAPITAL INVESTMENT PROJECTS

Types of capital investment projects a firm might undertake generally fall into five categories:

1. Replacement of totally obsolete equipment
2. Modernizing or replacing equipment for cost savings
3. Expanding existing product lines
4. Expansion into new product lines
5. Other

Replacement of totally obsolete equipment is straightforward. In order for operations to continue, new equipment must be purchased. While the cost of the equipment is important, it must be done regardless of potential savings or benefits.

The decision for modernizing, updating, or replacing equipment for cost savings and profit improvement may be made at various levels of management, depending upon the amount of money involved. You, as a supervisor or manager working close to the manufacturing operation, may provide the impetus to suggest capital investments for cost savings under this category. You may be asked to provide input needed in developing capital investment calculations for evaluating your proposal. Most of the discussion in the balance of this chapter involves evaluating and deciding on capital investment projects in this category.

Adding a new machine either for expansion of an existing product line or expanding into a new product line also involves capital equipment budgeting and requires development of capital investment calculations to justify expenditures. These project ideas generally originate at the division manager or other upper-level management levels. You may be asked for information to calculate the equipment and operating costs for these major changes. Capital decisions of the magnitude of a new plant or product line are infrequent.

Other types of capital investment would include items like the purchase and installation of mandatory pollution control equipment or a new telephone system. While these investments may take place at the factory level, they do not involve normal capital investment calculations since they do not involve savings and profits estimates as do most other capital investments.

CAPITAL BUDGETING

All capital expenditures are subject to review by upper-level management. Your company will have policies and procedures on paperwork required, an internal paperwork route, authority review of proposed expenditures, internal evaluation by the engineering and/or accounting departments, and internal cost-accounting procedures for gathering and reporting estimated costs and other necessary data.

Authority Review

For convenience, many companies will develop a schedule for management authority review based upon the cost of a proposed expenditure, i.e., approval of a capital expenditure can be made by managers (subject to review by the accounting department) at different administrative levels depending upon the costs involved. For example, you, as a supervisor or manager, could be authorized to purchase a capital item or authorize a capital-improvement project for $1,000 or less without prior approval of your supervisor. Any request above the $1,000 maximum would need approval by some higher level of management. In turn your supervisor might have authority without mandatory review up to $10,000. Your divisional manager might have authority up to $25,000 and so on. Even the president of your company would have some maximum level after which permission of the board of directors is required. You will need to know the authority levels in your company and the administrative chain of command. At what level of expenditure, for example, do you have to have your supervisor's permission to authorize a capital expenditure?

Paperwork—Proposals

For major capital expenditures top management may require a formal, written project proposal. A special form is not normally used. A formal proposal would include at least the following information:

1. Title of project

2. Description of project, including goals and objectives and place of project within corporate long-range plans

3. Proposed budget

4. Evaluation and justification, including capital-investment calculations

5. Proposed time lines, including targeted dates for beginning and ending the project.

Company policies and procedures are then followed in evaluating such proposals. Proposal development and evaluation will be discussed later in this chapter, after the introduction of capital-investment calculations and their uses.

Paperwork—Work-Order Forms

Capital improvement projects involving the maintenance department may be handled using a work-order system, a form of job-cost accounting. (The work-order form was discussed in Chapter 4, and shown in Exhibit 4–3.) The manager requesting the improvement completes a work-order form and submits the form to the maintenance department for the necessary administrative review.

As a minimum, the person filling out the work order provides the following information:

1. Department to be charged for the work

2. Cost center to be charged

3. Equipment number (assigned by engineering)

4. Description of the work required with justification for the request

5. Equipment required to be out of service during the job

6. Any potential hazards

7. Date of desired completion

8. Requester's name and date.

The work order is then passed for evaluation to the engineering department. The engineering department will complete estimated costs for labor, materials, and other costs and will recommend for or against capitalization. The work order is then passed through the necessary administrative chain of command for approval.

The work order is returned to the maintenance department for disposition. Once a capital-improvement project has been approved, the accounting department assigns the project a capital job number. All material, labor and other costs are then charged to the capital job number. The accounting department issues regular status summary reports to the requester for a designated time period (monthly, quarterly and yearly). These summary reports provide information needed to evaluate actual costs against budgeted costs, including variances. The requester must, of course, check to see that costs are reasonable and in line with the estimated budget.

Once the project has been completed, the accounting department closes the books on the job and sets up a depreciation schedule for charging depreciation on a periodic basis back to the cost center requesting the work.

CAPITAL-INVESTMENT CALCULATIONS

As noted earlier, evaluating capital-expenditure projects is a complex task due to the uncertainty managers must face in predicting future events. Yet good capital management is necessary for the long-term "health" of the corporation since large amounts of money are involved. Over the years, mathematical approaches have been developed in an attempt to provide objective, quantifiable criteria as an aid in judging the worth of large capital-equipment projects. You should understand some of these capital-investment calculations and their uses in evaluating capital-improvement projects.

Time Value of Money

In our United States economic system it is assumed, and rightfully so, that interest should be a positive number, so that a dollar today is worth more than a dollar in the future. That is, if you have excess cash today, you can invest it for some time period and, at a positive rate of interest, receive back more at the end of that time period than you invested. We quibble about the amount of the positive interest, not the fact that it will be positive.

Compound Interest

You are familiar with the use of compound interest from your own savings account. The mathematics of compound interest are straightforward.

If you invest $100 at 5 percent interest for one year, you will receive back your $100 investment plus a fee for the use of your money of $100 × .05, or $5. In a more general formula,

$$TV(1) = OI(1 + i)$$

where $TV(1)$ is the terminal value at the end of year 1, OI is the original investment, and i is the interest rate. For our example, $105 = $100 × 1.05.

If you invest the $100 for a two-year period, the interest for the second year is calculated at 5 percent of the $105 first-year balance for a $TV(2)$ of $110.25. In a more general formula,

$$TV(n) = OI(1 + i)^n,$$

where $TV(n)$ is the terminal value at the end of year n, OI is the original investment, and i is the interest rate. (Of course, you can compound more often than yearly and can change interest rates from year to year. This merely makes the formula more complex.) For our example, $110.25 = $100 × (1.05)^2.

To figure out what a dollar is worth at various interest

rates in future years, you can use special tables which have been developed for that purpose.

Present Values

The present-value concept is almost the reverse of the for-ward-compounding-interest concept. In its simplest sense, it determines how much you must invest today to receive a given amount at the end of a given period of time. For example, if you wish to have $100 one year from now, and interest is 5 percent, how much must you invest today? Using the general formula

$$TV(1) = OI(1 + i),$$

$$\$100 = OI(1 + .05) \text{ or } OI = 100/1.05 = \$95.24.$$

That is, to receive $100 at the end of one year, at 5 percent interest, you must invest $95.24. Thus, we say $95.24 today is worth $100 one year from now. In a more general formula,

$$OI = TV(n)/(1 + i)^n.$$

Again, present-value data can be conveniently looked up in standard tables, readily available in reference works. (You may discount back more frequently than once a year or at varying interest rates; it merely makes a slightly more complex problem.)

In a time period when interest rates are high, future income becomes heavily discounted back into today's dollars, i.e., you need to invest fewer dollars to have $100 a year from now. Dollars spent today are worth more than dollars spent in the future. On the other hand, your investments for the future will increase at a rapid rate. Consider, for example, all the advertisements about what Individual Retirement Accounts will be worth in forty years.

Capital costs (and their depreciation) are fixed costs. If we spend our dollars today, we must consider not only the present but the future value of the funds we invested.

CAPITAL-INVESTMENT TECHNIQUES

Although there are many capital-investment decision techniques, three are most commonly used by management. These are (1) the return on investment (ROI), (2) payback, and (3) the internal rate of return (IRR).

Return on Investment

The rate of return on investment is calculated by dividing the increased savings or profit by the amount of the investment.

$$\text{ROI} = \frac{\text{Increased savings or profit}}{\text{Investment}}$$

Savings or profit is calculated as cash flow, before depreciation and before taxes. For a project with a potential savings of $50,000 per year and an initial investment of $100,000, the ROI would be 50 percent per year.

$$\text{ROI} = \frac{50,000}{100,000} = .5 = 50\%$$

Payback

An alternate version of the ROI technique is called the payback period. The payback period is the number of years it takes a firm to recover its original investment from net cash flow. It is the inverse of the ROI.

$$\text{Payback} = \frac{\text{Investment}}{\text{Savings}}$$

Using the numbers from our example above, the project above would have a payback of two years. That is, we can say the cash flow from the first two years is used to reimburse the company for the investment. After two years, the cash flow is additional profit for the company.

$$\text{Payback period} = \frac{100,000}{50,000} = 2 \text{ years}$$

In its simplest form the ROI calculation assumes that the savings are the same per year, at least for the first few years. If this is not the case, the payback calculation can be more easily adjusted for uneven yearly savings. Consider an investment of $100,000 where the cash flows savings are:

Year	Cash Flow
1	$50,000
2	40,000
3	30,000
4	20,000
5	10,000

Thus, $90,000 of the $100,000 investment is paid back in the first two years, and the balance in the first third of the third year. The payback is thus two and one-third years.

Although an approximation, we could divide 100 percent by 2⅓ years to come up with an ROI of 43 percent over the payback years.

Both the ROI and the payback period calculations are reasonable when the ROI is high and the payback period is short. Both techniques ignore the time value of money and do not normally discount future cash flow back into today's dollars.

Internal Rate of Return (IRR)

The internal-rate-of-return calculation is a technique that takes into account the time value of money and gives the answer as a percentage value. The internal rate of return is defined as the interest rate that equates the present value of the expected future cash flows to the original cash outlay. As a formula:

$$\frac{F_1}{(1+r)^1} + \frac{F_2}{(1+r)^2} + \frac{F_3}{(1+r)^3} \cdots \frac{F_n}{(1+r)^n} - I = 0$$

where F_n is the funds flow in year n, I is the original investment, and r is the resultant interest rate.

The internal rate of return can be solved only by trial and error without a computer program. A manual calculation is shown in Exhibit 9–1, using the same variable savings data as above.

Thus, from the IRR calculation, discounting future flows back to the present, and considering flows after the original investment is paid back, the effective return on the original investment is 20 percent.

Comparison of Investment Techniques

Using the above example for discussion, we came up with 50 percent using the ROI technique, 43 percent using the inverse payback period, and 20 percent using the IRR technique. Which is correct? Answer: all of them! The issue is not the correctness of the answer but the way it is used.

EXHIBIT 9-1

Internal Rate of Return Example

For the manual calculation, an interest rate is approximated and plugged into the formula. For a start, 21% was selected:

$$\frac{50,000}{(1+r)^1} + \frac{40,000}{(1+r)^2} + \frac{30,000}{(1+r)^3} + \frac{20,000}{(1+r)^4} + \frac{10,000}{(1+r)^5} - 100,000 = 0$$

To calculate the details, you look up the present value of $1 at 21% in the appropriate year in a reference book table, and plug it into the table below.

Year	Amount	21% Factor	21% Amount	20% Factor	20% Amount
1	$50,000	.826	$41,300	.833	$41,650
2	40,000	.683	27,320	.694	27,760
3	30,000	.564	16,920	.579	17,370
4	20,000	.467	9,340	.482	9,640
5	10,000	.386	3,860	.402	4,020
	Total		$98,740		$100,440

For each year, you multiply the cash inflow by the appropriate discounting factor. For example, for year 1 $50,000 is multiplied by .826 for a discounted present value of $41,300. You repeat this multiplication for each year, and add the sums together.

Since the total cash inflow at 21% is too low ($98,740), you try a lower value, 20%. Looking up the factors at 20% and repeating the multiplication and addition gives a cash inflow of $100,400. Since this value is closer to $100,000 than $98,740, 20% is the internal rate of return that best satisfies the IRR equation.

The ROI technique is the most straightforward. If we are talking about relatively small amounts of money, and the percentage is high, then the investment will pay for itself over a very short time period, and there is no need to discount cash flow back to today's dollars. If we have uneven cash flows, or a medium time period (three to four years) is possible to pay back the investment, then the payback period is reasonable since, again, discounted cash flow is not necessary.

If, on the other hand, we are considering a large dollar investment, or an investment that will generate positive cash flows over a number of years, then a discounted technique like IRR offers advantages.

The choice of technique is less important than the use of a consistent technique and an understanding of how to interpret the results. Almost without exception the IRR technique will give a lower percentage than ROI or payback. In evaluating large capital-improvement proposals, management sets some minimum acceptable rate of return on investment, such as 12, 16, or 20 percent per year. Only those proposals which meet this minimum value, or hurdle, are considered for funding. As long as the managers making the final decisions are aware of the technique used, they can adjust their minimum hurdle, or threshold value, to be reasonable for the technique used. These problems will be discussed later in this chapter when talking about company capital-investment decision making.

RETURN ON INVESTMENT EXAMPLE

The supervisor of the metal-desk-fabricating department of the Harrisonburg Office Equipment Manufacturing Company has a problem. The sales department is complaining that the department cannot meet the demand for desks, and that this is causing customer complaints and lost profits. The department is currently working a three-shift, five-day-a-week schedule. Saturdays are being used for maintenance, and company policy suggests avoiding Sunday work if at all possible. The supervisor, the next-level manager, and the engineering manager review the department's operations and conclude that the department is being run efficiently to capacity. The supervisor checks further and finds that the bottleneck in the department is the presses that bend the sheet metal into the appropriate shape. While all of the presses are producing satisfactory-quality parts, one of the older presses produces substantially fewer parts per day than the other presses. Perhaps replacing this press with a newer press would allow the department to increase its output to a level satisfactory for the sales department. The question, however, is not simply increasing production. The real question is whether the profit produced by the additional sales is adequate to justify the expense of the new piece of equipment. This is the exact question the capital-investment techniques are designed to answer.

The Harrisonburg Office Equipment Manufacturing Company management has selected the return-on-investment calculation technique for capital decisions under $300,000 that offer paybacks in four years or sooner. Let's follow the steps to evaluate a potential new press for the department.

First, the department supervisor discusses the potential solution with the next-level manager. If that individual agrees, they ask the engineering and accounting departments for an investigation. Exhibits 9–2 through 9–5 detail the investigation.

The four exhibits are presented in that order because that is the order of the report that would be presented to

EXHIBIT 9-2

ROI Example—Summary Sheet

HARRISONBURG OFFICE EQUIPMENT
MANUFACTURING COMPANY
ESTIMATED RETURN ON INVESTMENT SUMMARY SHEET
JUNE 15, 198X
Requester: J. M. Smith
Project: New press, metal-desk fabricating department

Purchase of new press	$185,870	
Installation of new press	21,480	
Testing of new press	15,670	
Sale of old press	−18,000	
Removal of old press	13,740	
Total equipment capital investment		$218,760
Net increase in working funds		59,418
Total capital investment		278,178
Additional revenue		292,896
Additional cash costs		
Production costs	$157,296	
Maintenance	9,294	
Electricity	17,588	
Total cash costs		184,178
Net increase in profit		$108,718

$$ROI = \frac{Profit}{Investment} = \frac{\$108,718}{\$278,178} = .39 \text{ or } 39\%$$

---

upper-level management, with the summary sheet at the front. The discussion that follows lists the figures in the order in which you would actually perform the calculations. Study each figure first, then read the description below.

EXHIBIT 9-3

ROI Example—Capital-Equipment Costs

Purchase and Installation of New Press

---

1. New Press Purchase
The firm bid price for the new press delivered to your factory
is $185,870. This includes ten days for a vendor representative
to help with installation, setup, and "debugging."

2. New Press Installation
Because your maintenance force is already overloaded, the
vendor has quoted you a firm price of $21,480 for complete
installation. This includes all mechanical and electrical work,
including supervision. You have purchased equipment from
this vendor regularly and have found past work excellent.

3. Testing of New Press
You estimate it will take four weeks to debug the machine and
train employees to operate the machine on all three shifts.
The average wage rate for the employees involved, including
fringe benefits, is $10.73 per hour. 4 weeks × 40 hrs/week × 3
shifts = $5,150 labor costs. While material costs are harder to
estimate, your past history on other equipment has suggested
$10,520 of material will be scrapped during this process. Thus,
total testing and training costs are estimated at
$5,150 + $10,520 = $15,670.

Removal and Sale of Old Press

---

1. Purchase of Old Press
You have found a purchaser for your old press. This company
has offered you $18,000 for the old press delivered to it.

2. Removal of Old Press
Again, because of the unavailability of your own maintenance
people, you went out on bids and have a firm price quote of
$13,740 for complete removal, crating, and shipping of the
press to its new owner. You have dealt with the low bidder in
the past and have found their work very satisfactory.

EXHIBIT 9-4

ROI Example—Revenue and Cost Changes

Net Revenue Increase

Replacing the old press by a new press will allow you to increase output of the department by 7.2%. This will allow 226 additional units per month output. With an average selling price of $108 per unit, this will allow:

226 units per month × $108 per unit × 12 months = $292,896 additional revenue per year.

Production Variable Costs

The current variable cost per unit is $58. It is reasonable to assume that this will remain approximately the same with the new press added. Thus:

226 units per month × $58 × 12 months = $157,296 additional variable cost per year.

Maintenance Costs

While future maintenance costs are difficult to predict, our company has assumed 5% of the new-equipment capital cost a year is a reasonable amount, and this has been confirmed on past similar equipment. Thus:

$185,870 purchase price × .05 = $9,294 per year additional maintenance costs.

Additional Electricity Costs

The new press will use 250 horsepower motors, while the old press used only 125 horsepower. Thus, there will be a net increase of 125 horsepower. The average cost per horsepower the company buys from the electric company is $201 per year, and the company utility department estimates that 70% of its costs are variable costs. Thus:

125 HP × $201/HP × .70 = $17,588 per year additional.

EXHIBIT 9-5

ROI Example—Changes in Working Funds

Net Change in Working Funds

A reasonable assumption for the company is that an additional
month's worth of working funds will be required to support the
additional output. Working funds are made up of three components:

1. Accounts Receivable
   $108 per unit × 226 units per month = $24,408

2. Inventory
   $87 (full inventory cost) × 226 units per month = $19,662

3. Cost
   One month's out-of-pocket costs = $184,178/12 months
   = $15,348

Summary Increase in Working Funds

Accounts receivable	$24,408
Inventory	19,662
Cash	15,348
Total increase in working funds	$59,418

Exhibit 9-3 details the capital-equipment costs. The
engineering department investigates new presses and, with
advice from the department supervisor, selects particular
potential presses. Vendors are invited to submit fixed price
bids. The bids are evaluated, and a potential vendor selected.
(The selection will be based upon price, quality, and delivery, although opinion will play a part.) The price of the
selected press is $185,870. Since the maintenance depart-

ment is overworked, the engineering department asks the potential vendor for an installation quote. They give a firm price bid of $21,480. The department supervisor is consulted and estimates $15,670 to test and debug the new press and to train the necessary personnel. Meanwhile, the purchasing department has found a potential buyer of the old press at $18,000. The engineering department has contacted other vendors and obtained a low price bid of $13,740 to remove the old press and deliver it to the potential buyer.

Meanwhile, as shown in Exhibit 9–4, changes in revenue and cost are being estimated. With the new press, the overall increase in department output is estimated by the supervisor and engineering department at 7.2 percent. The other necessary equipment can absorb the additional production, although additional labor will be needed. Translated into units, the supervisor estimated that an additional 226 units per month can be produced. The sales department feels confident it can sell them all. At an average selling price of $108, the sales department estimates increased revenue of $292,896 per year from the new sales.

The additional production costs to consider are the variable costs, since the fixed costs are already being borne by the current production. The average variable cost for the metal desks produced are estimated by the accounting department at $58 per unit. Thus total additional production costs per year are $157,296. There are additional maintenance costs for the new press estimated at $9,294, and additional electrical costs of $17,588 from the larger demands of the new press.

While engineering and the department supervisor are gathering the above data, the accounting department is calculating the changes in working funds data shown in Exhibit 9–5. These working funds are the additional funds necessary to support the new production generated. Assuming most sales are made on credit, and billed and paid the next month, an additional $24,408 of accounts receivable will be generated. While there currently is no finished-goods inventory, a reasonable long-run approach cannot assume this condition will continue. Our company assumes that in the long run it will strive for one month's inventory of finished goods, and budgets $19,662 for cash to invest in this inventory. (Note that the appropriate cost value to place on inventory is the full average cost per unit, estimated by the accounting department at $87 per unit.) Finally, an additional cash need to support the production is estimated at one month's out-of-pocket cost, or $15,348. (This cash is one-twelfth of the additional yearly production, maintenance, and electricity costs. It assumes that you will pay these additional costs in cash each month.) Thus, a total increase in working funds of $59,418 is necessary to support the increased output generated by the new press.

Exhibit 9–2 summarizes the data gathered in Exhibits 9–3 to 9–5. Adding the price of the new press, the installation of the new press, the testing of the new press, the removal of the old press, and subtracting the sale price of the old press gives a total equipment capital investment of $218,760. Adding to this the increase in working funds of $59,418 gives a total capital investment of $278,178.

From additional sales of $292,896 are subtracted additional costs of $184,178 to give an increased profit before taxes and depreciation of $108,718.

Dividing the increased profit by the investment necessary to generate it gives a return on investment of 39 percent. Dividing 39 percent into 100 percent gives a payback period of 2.5 years.

CAPITAL INVESTMENT DECISION MAKING

With the 39 percent ROI the press should clearly be purchased, right? Well, maybe!

The calculation of an ROI value for a specific project is only the starting point in the decision-making process. In finance theory a firm should borrow money as long as the profit to be earned on the money is greater than the cost of borrowing the money. In practice, money is not borrowed individually for each project but for the overall company needs. In addition, the total amount of debt a firm can carry is limited. The practical fact is that there is only a limited amount of funds flow available each year for capital investment.

In general, there are many more requests for capital funds than there are funds available. Thus the problem becomes what specific projects from among the group of potential projects to select.

Major decisions on capital investment are made at the executive level. Company management will set some minimum, or threshold, or "hurdle," rate which a project must meet before it is considered. Once this minimum level has been met, other key factors come into play. These include the level of return, project life, risk, and importantly, general business conditions and requirements. In sum, once the hurdle has been met, a host of less readily quantifiable facts becomes the basis by which projects are reviewed for acceptance.

You as an operating supervisor or manager should constantly be looking for ways to improve operations. Even if proposed projects of yours have not been funded in the past, you should continue to suggest capital-investment ideas. Economic conditions change, and worthwhile projects may be denied funding due to no fault of the project or the person proposing the project.

In the case of our Harrisonburg Office Equipment Manufacturing Company press example, let us assume the company could borrow the money at 16 percent interest per year to finance the capital needed. Since the press's return is 39 percent, it is economically worthwhile. If the company does not desire the money for other, more profitable projects, and does want to expand its desk output, it should purchase the press.

LEASE VERSUS BUY

Companies obtain funds, either through borrowing or issuing equity, in order to acquire income-producing assets. Firms that are in business to produce goods and services are usually more interested in using the asset than in actual ownership. Leasing can be thought of as a specialized way of acquiring assets for use by a company without using the company's own funds to finance their purchase.

A lease is a contractual arrangement under which the owner of an asset (the lessor) permits another party (the lessee) to use the asset for a specified period of time in return for a specific payment. Although there are many variations in lease terms and obligations, the two types of leases encountered most often are operating and capital leases. Under an operating lease, the lessor is usually responsible for such things as maintenance, insurance, and property taxes. Computers and office equipment are typically covered by operating leases.

Capital leases, on the other hand, generally extend for longer terms, and the lessee may pay for maintenance, insurance, and property taxes. Normally, a capital lease will be set up in such a way that the lease payments fully pay for (depreciate) the original cost of the asset over the term of the lease, which may approximate the asset's useful life. In its Statement No. 13, the Financial Accounting Standards Board (a group that issues rules followed by most large firms and the Internal Revenue Service) requires that any lease which meets one or more of the following criteria be classified as a capital lease:

1. Ownership of the property is transferred to the lessee by the end of the lease.

2. The lease contains an option for the lessee to purchase the asset at less than fair market value.

3. The lease term is equal to 75 percent or more of the estimated economic life of the leased property.

4. The present value of payments required under the lease equals or exceeds 90 percent of the fair market value of the leased property.

All other leases are operating leases. The reason for this distinction is important and will be discussed shortly.

There are several reasons why a company might be motivated to lease rather than purchase an asset. First of all, leasing requires no substantial cash flow at the time of acquisition; the purchase option requires at least a large down payment. In addition, certain leases reduce the risk to the lessee in the event that the asset should become obsolete or have low resale value. But perhaps the biggest single factor which influences companies to lease is the fact that leasing offers certain timing, tax, and cash flow advantages which make it cheaper in the long run for the company to spread out an asset's cost over time rather than use its own funds to finance the purchase of the asset.

As an example, let us assume the Harrisonburg Office Equipment Manufacturing Company wishes to obtain an asset worth $5,000. The company may, of course, go out and purchase the asset with its own funds; however, it must be remembered that such funds are not "free" to the company. There are costs attached to company funds in the form of such things as interest on debt and dividends to stockholders. Let us assume that the cost of capital funds for our company is 16 percent after taxes. If the company buys the asset, depreciates it for five years (straight line), and sells it for $1,000 at the end of year 5, the actual flow of cash (assuming a 50 percent tax rate) can be calculated as shown in Exhibit 9–6.

It can be seen that the cash purchase has no effect on taxes; however, the depreciation of the asset in years 1 through 4 results in tax avoidances of $500 per year. (In the last year the gain on the sale of the asset exactly offsets the depreciation, and there is no net tax effect.)

Similarly, if the company acquires the same $5,000 asset through leasing for $1,300 per year, it is, in effect, financing the asset with someone else's money. Since this is an operating lease, the entire lease payment may be treated as an expense for tax purposes giving the net cash flow figures shown in Exhibit 9–6.

After figuring the net cash flow for each option, the company's time value of money must be taken into consideration. In our example, our purpose is to find the cheapest way to acquire a $5,000 asset, so you multiply by the appropriate present value factor for our 16 percent cost of capital. The resulting figures are expressed in "today's" dollars, and the sum of the present value of all cash outflows and inflows is called the net present value.

The purpose of comparing the purchase and lease options in Exhibit 9–6 is to try to select the method for acquiring the asset which will result in the lowest net present value of cash outflow. The fact that the lease option appears cheaper than the purchase option by $997 derives from several factors. First, because of the time value of money, a dollar invested today always costs more than a dollar invested at a later date. The purchase option requires that the machine be paid for with $5,000 of today's dollars, whereas the lease option spreads the payments out over several future periods. Even though the simple sum of the lease payments is $6,500, the timing of the payments is

EXHIBIT 9-6

Lease-versus-Purchase Comparison

A-Purchase Option*

Year	0	1	2	3	4	5
Purchase	5,000					
Depreciation		(1,000)	(1,000)	(1,000)	(1,000)	(1,000)
Gain on sale						1,000
		(1,000)	(1,000)	(1,000)	(1,000)	–0–
Less tax avoidance		500	500	500	500	---
		(500)	(500)	(500)	(500)	–0–
+ Depreciation**		1,000	1,000	1,000	1,000	1,000
Net cash flow	(5,000)	500	500	500	500	1,000
× present value factor @ 16%†	1.00	.862	.743	.641	.552	.476
Present value	(5,000)	431	372	320	276	476

Total net present value = $(3,125)

B-Lease Option

Year	0	1	2	3	4	5
Lease payment		(1,300)	(1,300)	(1,300)	(1,300)	(1,300)
Less tax savings		650	650	650	650	650
Net cash flow	–0–	(650)	(650)	(650)	(650)	(650)
× present value factor @ 16%	1.00	.862	.743	.641	.552	.476
Present value	–0–	(560)	(483)	(417)	(359)	(309)

Total net present value = $(2,128)

Advantage of leasing vs. purchasing = $3,125 – $2,128 = $997

*Assumptions:
   —50% Corporate tax bracket
   —16% Cost of capital
   —Straight-line depreciation of the asset in question over five years
**Because depreciation does not involve an actual cash outflow, it is expensed
   for tax purposes only and then added back to determine the final cash flow.
†present value factor taken from an appropriate reference book

more favorable, given our cost of capital. In this particular case, it is cheaper to let someone else own the asset and worry about financing the purchase with their own funds.

This example illustrates the fundamentals of setting up a lease/buy analysis. There are, however, many more complex forms of leasing than the one shown here. For example, capital leases are treated differently for tax purposes. Under a capital lease, an asset is carried on the company's balance sheet and depreciated for tax purposes as if it had been purchased. In this case only the interest portion of the lease payment may be deducted. Details of the calculations for capital leasing can be found in a number of references in the bibliography.

PROJECT
BUDGETING

*"How do program or project budgets
differ from operating budgets?"*

WHAT IS A PROJECT BUDGET?

Project budgets are developed for projects or programs which
are generally one-time, long-term commitments involving
the expenditure of large amounts of money. Project budgets
differ from operating budgets in that project budgets may
extend over a period of years. Two major areas in which
project budgets are used are in the development of major
capital assets and in research and development projects.
Examples of project planning and budgeting are planning
and budgeting for the construction of a new building, the
development and testing of a new product line, a research
and development project, or filling a government contract.

We have discussed the planning cycle for developing
and selecting capital projects in detail in Chapter 9. Planning
and budgeting in project management can be complex due
to the size of the project and the extended time period over
which the project is completed. Upper-level management

may spend a great deal of time and energy in planning, scheduling, and budgeting for projects. In developing a project budget, management will develop procedures for estimating, gathering data on, and controlling costs, for monitoring the rate of progress of the project, and for evaluating quality control.

PLANNING FOR PROJECT IMPLEMENTATION

Generally, the project manager will first develop a master schedule which will be used to schedule project activities, to monitor progress in meeting deadlines for project completion, and to estimate, collect, analyze, and evaluate costs associated with the project. For this purpose, the project manager will break up the job into the major activities which need to be accomplished, and these activities into more detailed sub-activities. For example, if we are building a new plant in order to increase production capabilities, we could break the work to be done into a series of major activities or tasks, such as location and purchase of land, architectural design of the new plant, erection of the building, and purchase and installation of equipment.

These major activities can then be sub-divided into more and more specific sub-activities. In erecting the building, for example, we must define all the sub-tasks required to complete this portion of the project. Some sub-tasks would be laying gas lines, laying water lines, excavating for the foundation, and laying the foundation. Thus a major task will be broken down into many smaller, more manageable work packages. As an operating manager, you may be involved in project management when you are assigned the responsibility for completing one or more packages within the project.

ORGANIZATIONAL STRUCTURE

In project management, companies may use different organizational structures for different projects. For example, management may assign a project manager the full responsibility for all aspects of the project. Employees working on the project are assigned directly to the project manager. In other instances, management may appoint a project manager who supervises the overall project while departmental (functional) managers in the company are responsible for completion of work assigned to their cost centers (matrix management).

SCHEDULING FOR PROJECT MANAGEMENT

Times for initiating and completing each major activity or task are generally scheduled using some systematic techniques developed over the years specifically for that purpose. One example of such techniques is the use of bar charts, called Gantt charts, on which activities are charted graphically against a simplified monthly or weekly calendar.

Use of planning charts and work packages simplifies the budgeting process and provides a means for evaluating the progress of project completion. For complex projects sophisticated mathematical techniques, such as the Critical Path Method (CPM) or the Program Evaluation and Review Technique (PERT) may be used to analyze and schedule activities. You can consult titles in the bibliography for detailed descriptions of these techniques.

DEVELOPING PROJECT BUDGETS

Once work packages have been developed and coordinated, the project manager will identify responsibility centers for doing the required work packages. The project manager should meet with the functional managers to explain the work breakdowns, departmental responsibilities, the time elements involved for each stage of the project, and the quality of work expected. At this meeting, the project and functional managers may identify problems which need to be resolved. Functional managers may in turn meet with their own operating supervisors or managers to establish guidelines and assign tasks.

Functional managers of these responsibilty centers may be asked to develop estimates of direct and indirect costs (that is, a budget) required to complete the work assigned to their cost centers. Your supervisor may ask you to develop a portion of the departmental budget for work packages to be performed by your area. You may be asked to supply the number of labor hours by types of labor required, materials estimates, and other costs for each month of work-package activities. It is important that the cost data you supply be as accurate as possible. As in the development of your operating budget, you may use historical data from your previous operations or engineering standards, as available and applicable to the work to be done, in developing the budget for your assigned work packages.

In project management, time is indeed money. Each level of management needs to be aware of the importance of meeting project deadlines at each level of the planning, budgeting, and implementation stages for the project. It is important that you be aware of the time constraints on filling your work packages, since you will be under pressure to complete the work at an acceptable level of quality within the planned time period. You will need to develop your labor estimates with time constraints in mind. For example, uneven work flows may cause problems in scheduling the labor hours to be worked. Any problems which you may anticipate should be brought to the attention of your supervisor.

Once your departmental budget has been submitted for all the work packages to be filled, the project manager may come back to your supervisor with questions or requests for changes in the proposed budget. For example, suppose that to meet the time schedule you had to schedule a great deal of overtime, increasing the cost of the work. If the project manager feels the costs are too high, you can decrease the costs, provided the project manager is willing to let the work package time stretch out. Some negotiation may be necessary between the functional managers and the project manager. Your supervisor should involve you in the negotiation if your cost center is involved. In any case, you should be kept informed by your supervisor of any changes which will affect your cost center.

After gathering all costs, including the allocation of a portion of fixed costs, such as administration costs, rent, and custodial services, the project manager will then assemble these estimates for all of the work packages and develop monthly, quarterly, and annual budgets for the project. At the project level, project budgets, as developed by the project manager, may differ from operating budgets in that critical points in time, money, and other resources which must be met if the project is to fall within acceptable profitability ranges are included in the budget. The project manager will also have a budget for each work package to be completed by the various cost centers.

As in normal budgeting practices, the accounting department will collect actual costs for each cost center just as it does for operating budgets. Project budgeting differs from operating budgets in that costs are also collected against a project number, assigned by the accounting department. In effect, a project cost system is similar to that employed in a job-cost accounting system. A paperwork flow will be used to collect costs against the cost centers and the project number. Time cards or time sheets, purchase orders, and material requisitions are used as cost records. (As an operating manager, you have the responsibility for keeping accurate, timely time sheets and other paperwork for your assigned work packages.) Actual costs are then collected for each work package by assigning costs through the paperwork flow both to a cost center and to a project number as well.

THE OPERATING CYCLE

Different methods may be used in controlling the actual operations cycle in project management. Generally, some paperwork authorization system will be established to authorize the performance of work packages by cost centers. A work-authorization form, such as that shown in Exhibit 10–1, may be used to assign specific charge numbers to cost centers by work packages.

As an example, Exhibit 10–1 shows a work-authorization form for work-package number 90–1341, "Install new punch press in department C-28," one sub-activity of the project titled Plant Addition. Three internal departments have been asked for their estimates of labor hours and materials to complete their portion of the work. Their estimates have been acceptable to the project manager, or any differences have been worked out. In addition, skills were not available inside the company for all the work, so outside bids were solicited. The bids were reviewed, and two firm price contracts issued for part of the work. After the planning is complete, the project manager issues this work-authorization form as the authority to actually carry out the work.

EXHIBIT 10-1

Project Work Authorization Form

WORK-AUTHORIZATION FORM

Project: PLANT ADDITION   Work-Package Number 90-1341

Date of original issue: March 1, 198X
Date of revision: Revision number:

Work Description	Cost Center	Labor Hours	Mate-rials	Start Date	Finish Date
	C-3	175	$345	4-1	5-16
Install new	C-6	65	910	4-6	5-16
punch press	C-8	45	0	5-1	5-16
in department	C-99-15*	0	2,150	4-1	4-16
C-28	C-99-16*	0	1,235	4-8	4-25

*C-99 is the cost center for outside contractors. The code numbers 15 and 16 after the cost center identify the vendor. Notice that dollar amounts, not hours, are listed. This indicates that the costs are firm price quotes, not labor-hour estimates.

Note that the date on the authorization is March 1, far enough in advance of the April 1 start date so that the cost-center supervisors can integrate this work package into their other work. When the work is actually carried out, the actual costs will be assigned to both the cost center and the work-package number.

Cost centers are authorized to charge costs against charge numbers only for the period specified by the work authorization. The beginning and completion dates specify the time period when the work package is to be accomplished. All costs are then accumulated against the specified cost centers and the work-package number. In general, the labor hours listed are the maximum that may be charged. The charging of labor hours beyond this maximum would require written authorization from the project manager. The functional manager of the cost center involved in the request would initiate the paperwork on standard forms provided for this purpose by project management. The functional manager will be required to justify the reasons for the increased budget request. You will be responsible for completing the work package assigned to your cost center within the time period specified and within the budgeted labor hours. If any problems should develop, you should discuss them with your supervisor immediately. Accounting may prepare a labor-hours weekly summary report for the project manager and the appropriate functional managers so that potential problems can be identified quickly.

COST-CONTROL MEASURES

The accounting department will accumulate actual costs from each cost center at each level of project activity, with a total project budget report produced. Periodically, the accounting department will issue a variance statement for project costs which will include the current reporting-period costs and the cumulative costs to date. Variance reports for actual costs at each individual cost center and at each work-package number will also be produced. Thus, managers at each level of activity will be responsible for analyzing variances between budgeted and actual costs for work packages under their control as a cost-control method for the project. You will receive a budget report for the work packages done by your cost center. You will be responsible for conducting a variance analysis, just as you do for your operating budget.

The cost-center variance-analysis report will be similar to the example discussed in detail in Chapter 7. Exhibit 10–

EXHIBIT 10-2

Project Variance-Analysis Report

Project:
PLANT ADDITION
Work-Package Number 90-1341
JUNE 10, 198X

Cost Center	May				Work Package to Date*			
	Budget	Actual	Variance	%	Budget	Actual	Variance	%
C-3	$ 991	$1,015	$(24)	(2)	$2,392	$2,597	$(205)	(9)
C-6	477	613	(136)	(29)	1,742	2,014	(272)	(16)
C-8	1,013	857	156	15	1,013	857	156	15
C-99-15	0	0	0	0	2,150	2,150	0	0
C-99-16	0	0	0	0	1,235	1,235	0	0
Total	$2,481	$2,485	$(4)	(0)	$8,532	$8,852	$(321)	(4)

*Work Package 90-1341 completed in May, 198x

2 shows an example of a work-package variance-analysis report for number 90–1341, the example shown in Figure 10–1.

From Exhibit 10–1, the labor hours are translated into dollars, and labor dollars and material dollars are assigned to April and May as they are expected to be used. On June 10, a variance-analysis report for May and for the work package to date is issued.

In Exhibit 10–2, the actual costs for May and the work package to date are compared to the actual costs and both a dollar variance and percentage variance calculated. Thus, for May, cost center C-6 was over budget by 29 percent, but overall the total cost was on target. For the work package to date (actually the end of the work package), all cost-center actual costs were close to the budgeted amounts, showing an excellent job of budgeting and cost control.

These individual work-package variance reports should be combined into an overall project variance report. The project manager, in cooperation with the functional managers, will be responsible for explaining any large variance between budgeted and actual costs. The project manager will use these budget analyses to evaluate actual versus planned costs as a cost-control measure, similar to the way you evaluate your own budget reports. During this process, the project manager will also evaluate the actual time taken to accomplish the work done against the scheduled time allotted to the work on the project schedule. Again, as a manager or supervisor involved in a project cycle, you must remember that you have objectives to meet not only in terms of expected output and cost controls but in time constraints as well.

If a flexible budgeting system is being used, the project manager may have to develop revised budgets on the basis of actual data in order to reflect current estimates of schedule, costs, and technical performance.

BUDGETING
FOR NON-PROFIT
ORGANIZATIONS

"What are the budgeting differences
in non-profit organizations?"

DIFFERENCES BETWEEN PROFIT AND NON-PROFIT ORGANIZATIONS

The obvious difference between a profit and a non-profit organization is that non-profit organizations are not designed to distribute profits to stockholders or owners. A non-profit organization is organized to provide some services. Financing the non-profit organization may be done by the community or group it serves, or by some outside agency, like the federal government. Non-profit organizations range from small, local organizations, such as your local school district, church, social club, public library, or S.P.C.A., to large organizations (national or international in scope), such as the U.S. Chamber of Commerce, U.S. Postal Service, American Management Associations, or American Cancer Society. The influence of non-profit organizations is felt in every sector of society in areas such as government, education, religion, politics, health, and recreation. Together, their programs account for the expenditure of billions of dollars in the nation's economy. No matter whether an organization is organized as a profit or non-profit enterprise, one financial formula is basic in accounting procedures:

$$\text{Profit} = \text{Revenue} - \text{Costs}$$

Although non-profit organizations do not distribute profits as dividends to stockholders, this formula still applies. Non-profit organizations generally must strive for a profit of zero. Few organizations, other than some agencies such as the U.S. Postal Service, can continue to operate with deficits. In non-profit accounting, the terms "surplus" or "deficit" are normally used instead of "profit" or "loss." Some non-profit organizations do generate surplus funds or "profits" to be used for purchase of capital items or to provide a financial cushion for "rainy days." The amount of surplus funds which can be retained is limited by law, if an organization is to maintain its non-profit status.

Another way in which many non-profit organizations differ is that the organization may have to operate within a fixed income; that is, the approved budget is the maximum amount the organization can spend. Many such agencies are funded by federal, state, or local governments. Frequently, these agencies by law are required to return any surplus funds provided by their governing bodies at the end of the fiscal year. Other non-profit organizations are dependent upon the willingness of members to provide revenues to support the organization through contributions, dues, or pledges. Churches and civic and professional organizations fall into this category.

The accounting system for many small non-profit organizations usually is designed simply to account for expenditures, not to provide a basis for planning and control. The treasurer or other finance officer may prepare an annual budget at the beginning of each fiscal year, but the budget is ignored once it has been approved by the governing body of the organization. For this reason, the treasurer simply records revenue and costs using a cash method, rather than the accrual method used by most profit enterprises. This is poor practice in most instances. All, except the very smallest non-profit organizations should use the accrual system so that income and expenses can be matched for accounting and cost-control purposes. A cash balance cannot provide an accurate record of where an organization stands in terms of accounts receivable and accounts payable.

NEED FOR
PLANNING AND CONTROL

Non-profit organizations, like their profit counterparts, need to have a planning and cost-control system. The administration needs to plan so that the activities of the organization can be selected, organized, and implemented in such a way as to maximize attainment of the organization's goals, that is, its purpose for existence, in as economical a manner as possible. Systematic planning (as discussed in Chapter 2), both in the long- and short-term, will provide a framework for decision making in which proposed services and costs can be evaluated. As in profit enterprises, clear statements of goals by the board of directors and upper-level administrators provide input to department heads, employees, or volunteers as a framework for planning. Once goals have been established, department heads or chairpersons at the operational level should bear at least some responsibility in developing clearly stated operating objectives to be accomplished during the year—what tasks are to be achieved and what costs are to be expected. This planning forms the foundation for developing the operating budget.

A cost-accounting system (as described in earlier chapters) will provide control over expenditures as a means of minimizing the chance of spending beyond the budget allotted. Comparison of expected revenues and costs with actual revenue and costs can pinpoint potential problems which require administrative action. Savings incurred through effective cost controls may generate opportunities to:

1. Expand services being offered.

2. Increase the number of users of given services.

3. Provide surplus funds for future needs.

4. Generate surplus funds for purchase of capital items.

5 Allow surplus funds to be returned to the governing body (possibly local, state, and federal governments) to decrease the costs associated with that body.

PLANNING

The systematic planning model discussed in Chapter 2 serves as the basis for planning in non-profit organizations as well. To begin the planning process, the administration develops a long-range plan from which specific, quantifiable short-term objectives will be generated. During this process the administration should evaluate and review all ongoing programs to determine if they should be continued. New programs should be considered in light of today's rapidly changing society. Capital expenditure requirements for both the long and short term should be identified.

Once specific objectives by program have been identified, alternative strategies for achieving objectives are evaluated. Department heads and other professionals in the organization should be involved in the decision-making process, in developing annual objectives, alternative strategies, and budget preparation. Once programs have been identified, specific objectives clarified, and a plan of action developed, the budgeting process can begin. This planning is important since many costs incurred by non-profit organizations are discretionary based upon the administration's decisions to spend funds.

THE BUDGETING CYCLE

The budgeting cycle may vary from organization to organization. The following steps constitute a typical budget cycle:

1. Each program or department head develops and submits a budget request for review by the administration, based upon the objectives for program or department. (Remember that such objectives must be quantifiable.) If costs do not vary widely from month to month, quarterly and annual budgets may be adequate. If costs are highly variable, monthly, quarterly, and annual budgets are submitted. These requests would constitute a line-item budget for each department or program, with appropriate lines for items like salaries, travel, and supplies. Capital-equipment needs should be identified, along with appropriate cost figures, justification, and statement of proposed savings. The administration should establish firm time lines, in the form of a calendar, for the submission and review process. Budget guidelines, such as percentage of anticipated cost increases for standard items, should be given to department heads when available. Since this process is time-consuming, department heads should receive sufficient planning time to accomplish the task.

2. The treasurer or other financial officer combines these departmental annual budgets to form a tentative annual budget for the organization. In independent organizations which are not funded by outside agencies, the financial officer should develop a schedule of expected revenue for the next fiscal year. Estimated revenue should be conservative, if the organization has no surplus funds to serve as an emergency cash reserve. The statement of expected revenue will serve as the maximum allowed for proposed costs for the year.

3. The budget committee should meet with department heads to amend or revise the proposed budget. Once departmental budgets have been agreed upon and the complete budget approved, the chief administrator of the organization may be called upon to "sell" the proposed budget to some governing agency. Here a final budget is approved and funds authorized for the fiscal period.

4. Once funding has been set, departmental budgets or program budgets may need to be revised to reflect actual funding. Systematic planning has the advantage of reducing the problems which are encountered in readjusting the operating budgets, since expenses may be evaluated using a priority system.

COST-ACCOUNTING SYSTEM

In developing the organization's cost-accounting system the accrual system should be used, so that revenue and costs can be "matched." Using the accrual system, monthly, quarterly, and yearly budget reports (as needed) can be developed to provide a method for determining variances between expected and actual revenue and costs. (If budget reports are not available, the previous year's revenue and cost figures can be used as a cost-comparison base.)

Variance reports are most useful when actual variances are expressed in both dollar and percentage differences between expected and actual costs. Current month (or quarter) and year-to-date revenue and costs should be included on the variance report. The financial officer should issue variance reports on a timely basis, within at least three weeks from the end of the budget period (month, quarter, and annual). Once variance reports have been received, department heads or chairpersons are then responsible for explaining any large variances in the budget. They should develop and present to the administration a written report analyzing large variances and suggesting solutions if problems are identified.

In order to provide budget reports, balance sheets, and other financial statements, a paperwork flow, similar to that employed in industry, is necessary. Account numbers are assigned to each department, program, or committee. Each account number will identify the department and the type of expense. For example, department A (as a cost center) will have account number A100 to identify salaries for department A. Department B salaries will be charged to B100, and so on. A voucher system with appropriate account number is used for purchase of goods and services. This system will also provide an audit trail for the organization.

NON-PROFIT DEPRECIATION ACCOUNTING

The treatment of fixed-asset capitalization and depreciation has undergone changes over the last few years. In the past, many non-profit organizations have written off their fixed-asset purchases as current cost rather than capitalize and depreciate them. They did this because many administrators did not feel matching revenues and costs was important. As the accounting societies have advised more and more non-profit organizations to move to an accrual accounting system from a cash system, it becomes necessary to capitalize fixed assets and depreciate them over a number of years. (Non-profit organizations may depreciate assets over longer time periods than profit companies, however, since the tax considerations of depreciation do not play a part in the decisions of non-profit organizations.) An accurate cost-accounting system requires that assets be capitalized and depreciated; otherwise the accounting system does not provide accurate costs of the services provided.

THE SHENVALL PROFESSIONAL ASSOCIATION—AN EXAMPLE

Examples of non-profit organizations range from giant organizations like the American Cancer Society to small organizations like a local Special Olympics committee. No example can cover all facets of all organizations. We have chosen as a practical example of the application of a budgeting system a hypothetical professional association. Our Shenvall Professional Association is typical of many non-profit organizations in business, education, and other areas, where a group of people have organized to provide ongoing training in a field, to disseminate information of interest to the membership, and to provide leadership in areas affecting the welfare of the membership. This example will serve to represent all the aspects of non-profit budgeting.

The Shenvall Professional Association is a hypothetical statewide organization of professionals. (It could be a group of accountants, librarians, or surveyors.) Membership has grown over the last fifteen years to approximately 1,100 dues-paying members. The organization's goals are broadly educational in nature. Its purpose is to provide current information to its members through provision of conferences and meetings and publication of a quarterly newsletter, a membership directory, and other occasional publications. The organization also has as its goal the provision of leadership on issues affecting standards for the profession. It has several standing committees for this purpose. The association has no costs for salaries or headquarters, since it is run purely by volunteers.

In the past the organization has generated a surplus and has accumulated some $15,000 in cash reserves in a savings account. At the end of year 198x − 2, the association found it had a cash deficit of $3,000 for the year. The board of directors was concerned and decided to switch to an accrual accounting system and to institute a planning and control program to attempt to reduce costs and pinpoint problem areas. Since the board was not in a panic situation, it decided to follow the framework outlined earlier in this chapter, and develop a budget for the 198x year. In July of year 198x − 1, the treasurer developed the budgets shown in Exhibits 11–1 and 11–2, and they had been approved by the board.

Exhibit 11–1 shows expected revenue for the 198x year. Because the revenue is straightforward, it was felt that monthly budgets were not necessary and that quarterly budgets were more practical. Revenues were estimated in each of the four major categories and summed to give yearly totals. (Note that no miscellaneous income was estimated, although there will be some contributions during the year. Since no basis is available to make the estimate, we followed the conservative approach of estimating zero miscellaneous revenue.) Thus, total income of $20,951 was estimated. Because the annual conference is in October, many members joined at that time and have paid dues in the last quarter of the year ever since. Thus, the revenue is not smooth over the year, with 50 percent being received in the last quarter.

Exhibit 11–2 shows expected costs for the 198x year. Again, costs are estimated quarterly and summed into the five major categories shown. These quarterly costs are summed to a yearly cost estimate. Notice that overall rev-

EXHIBIT 11-1

Yearly Budgeted Revenue, Year 198X

SHENVALL PROFESSIONAL ASSOCIATION
BUDGETED REVENUE, YEAR 198X
JULY 20, 198X – 1

	First Quarter	Second Quarter	Third Quarter	Fourth Quarter
Dues	$2,400	$2,400	$3,600	$4,800
Newsletter	292	292	875	292
Checking interest	50	50	50	50
Conference	0	0	0	5,800
Miscellaneous	0	0	0	0
Total	$2,742	$2,742	$4,525	$10,942

Yearly Totals

Dues	$13,200
Newsletter	1,751
Checking interest	200
Conference	5,800
Miscellaneous	0
Total revenue	$20,951

enue is estimated at $20,951 and overall costs at $20,149, so a budget surplus of $802 is estimated. Costs are reasonably spread out over the year, since member services are spread over the year; newsletters go out quarterly, and many of the yearly conference costs are paid out in quarters prior to the conference.

Thus, even though the association plans a surplus, it will have to dip into its cash reserves to cover cash flow until the fourth quarter.

EXHIBIT 11-2

Yearly Budgeted Operating Costs, Year 198X

SHENVALL PROFESSIONAL ASSOCIATION
BUDGET OF OPERATING COSTS, YEAR 198X
JULY 20, 198X – 1

	First Quarter	Second Quarter	Third Quarter	Fourth Quarter
Conferences	$ 500	$ 500	$1,000	$2,300
Administration	765	880	765	765
Publications	1,000	1,000	2,500	1,000
Committees	1,787	1,987	788	788
Computer	250	250	250	250
Miscellaneous	206	206	206	206
Total	$4,508	$4,823	$5,509	$5,309

Yearly Totals

Conferences	$4,300
Administration	3,175
Publications	5,500
Committees	5,350
Computer	1,000
Miscellaneous	824
Total costs	$20,149

As the association moved into 198x, a quarterly variance analysis was carried out. The first quarter variance analysis in year 198x showed revenue much lower than expected, and the variance analysis for the second quarter showed the trend continuing. The variance analysis at the end of the second quarter is shown in Exhibit 11–3.

Exhibit 11–3 is a typical variance analysis as discussed in detail in Chapter 7. The budgeted versus actual revenue is listed, and the variance calculated. Note that when actual revenue is less than budgeted revenue, the difference is considered a negative variance (in parentheses). That is, where actual revenue is less than budgeted, the organization has a potential problem; identifying the variance as negative more clearly shows the variance as a potential problem. The budgeted versus actual costs are also listed, and the variance is listed. Note here that a negative variance (in parentheses) indicates actual cost greater than budgeted costs, again indicating a potential problem. Finally, the surplus or deficit is calculated, again with the deficit in parentheses indicating a negative number. By designing the variance report this way, positive variances can be looked upon as generally favorable, and negative variances as generally unfavorable.

At the end of the first six months of the fiscal year, revenue is down from what was budgeted by $2,072, or 38 percent. This was because of dues being 48 percent under what was expected. Costs were $380, or 4 percent, less than were budgeted. The net result is that where a $3,847 deficit was budgeted, the actual deficit was $5,539, or 44 percent, more than was budgeted.

In preparing the variance-analysis report, the treasurer included budgeted revenue and costs, actual costs, dollar variances and percentage of variance. You should analyze any large variances, say any variance above 20 percent. Since dues constitute the primary source of income, the negative variance on dues income should be of great concern. As noted above, by the end of the six-month period, revenue from dues is 48 percent lower than expected. A minor bright spot is that revenue from newsletter advertising is 21 percent higher than expected. Conference costs are running higher than anticipated during the first six months. Someone should investigate the cause! Overall, however, total costs for the first six-month period have been $380 lower than estimated.

The treasurer knew that the organization had to get back

EXHIBIT 11–3

Variance Analysis, First Six Months, 198X

SHENVALL PROFESSIONAL ASSOCIATION
REVENUE AND COST VARIANCE ANALYSIS,
YEAR 198X
JULY 20, 198X

| | Second Quarter | | | Six Months | | |
	Budget	Actual	Variance	%	Budget	Actual	Variance	%
Revenue:								
Dues	$2,400	$1,040	($1,360)	(57%)	$4,800	$2,520	($2,280)	(48%)
Newsletter	292	355	63	22%	584	709	125	21%
Interest	50	52	2	4%	100	110	10	10%
Conference	0	0	0	0	0	0	0	0
Miscellaneous	0	25	25	—	0	73	73	—
Total	$2,742	$1,472	($1,270)	(46%)	$5,484	$3,412	($2,072)	(38%)

	Second Quarter				Six Months			
	Budget	Actual	Variance	%	Budget	Actual	Variance	%
Costs:								
Conference	$ 500	$ 862	($362)	(72%)	$1,000	$1,621	($621)	(62%)
Administration	880	745	135	15%	1,645	1,327	318	19%
Publications	1,000	837	163	16%	2,000	1,674	326	16%
Computer	250	250	0	0	500	525	(25)	(5%)
Committees	1,987	2,019	(32)	(2%)	3,774	3,315	459	12%
Miscellaneous	206	350	(144)	(70%)	412	489	(77)	(19%)
Total	$4,823	$5,063	($240)	(5%)	$9,331	$8,951	$380	4%
Surplus (Deficit)	($2,081)	($3,591)	($1,510)	(73%)	($3,847)	($5,539)	($1,692)	(44%)

in the black and that a budget had to be developed for year
198x + 1. At the next board of directors meeting the treasurer
brought up the problem. The board then decided to institute
a planning and control program to attempt to reduce costs
and pinpoint problem areas.

During this planning process, the board gained insight
into some specific problems which should receive board
action. Problems readily apparent are:

1. The need for an active policy to encourage membership
    renewal and procedures regarding purging of non-
    renewals from the membership list

2. The need to evaluate the entire membership structure
    used by the membership committee in billing, main-
    taining membership files, and recruiting for new mem-
    bers

3. The existence of a cash flow problem. The bulk of the
    association's revenue is receivable in the last half of the
    year. As a possible solution, the treasurer suggested that
    some members be asked to pay prorated dues, so that
    future renewals would be spread out more evenly
    throughout the year.

(One problem inherent in such organizations is the lack
of continuity in program and financial planning. Elected
officers and board members may change over a yearly or
biennial period. The administration which prepares a budget
for membership approval may be replaced by a new administration which has had little input into the process.
Hence, although problems may be identified, no consistent
plan is ever developed and implemented on a long-term
basis.)

It was clear from the analysis of Exhibit 11–3 that the
major immediate financial problem is the non-renewal of
membership by existing members. Dues from members con-

stituted 80 percent of the association's revenue. In its analysis, the board found that membership records were not up-to-date, with many members not paying dues. Thus, the board set up a plan where over the next few months the membership records were organized using a monthly due-date system. A renewal notice will now be sent out the month the dues are payable. Another problem was that non-paying members had not been purged from the membership rolls. This meant that variable and semi-variable costs were increased since these non-payers were still receiving newsletters and other correspondence, which increased costs. It was agreed that non-payers would be purged after two reminder letters, approximately three months after their dues expired.

In addition to these changes, the board agreed to raise yearly dues from $12 to $15, and to increase the conference fees to increase revenues.

Based upon these changes, the treasurer was able to start the budget process to plan the 198x + 1 yearly budget.

Exhibit 11–4 shows the result of the budget process with the approved revenue budget for 198x + 1.

Income from dues was estimated on the basis of percentage of memberships dues per quarter, since the treasurer did not expect the new prorating system to be set up that quickly. The membership of 1,100 broke down into 200 renewals in quarter 1, 200 in quarter 2, 300 in quarter 3, and 400 in quarter 4. Thus, as shown in Figure 11–4, first-quarter income was projected as 200 members × $15 or $3,000. Advertising revenue from the association's newsletter was estimated at $1,751 in the current year. Although the board established a goal of increasing revenues from newsletter advertising, members decided to be conservative in its income estimation. A projected income of $1,751 from newsletter advertising was used in the budget estimate for the next fiscal year. Also, in analyzing the previous year's income and expenses, the treasurer reported that advertising

EXHIBIT 11-4

Yearly Budgeted Revenue, Year 198X + 1

SHENVALL PROFESSIONAL ASSOCIATION
BUDGETED REVENUE, YEAR 198X + 1
JULY 20, 198X

	First Quarter	Second Quarter	Third Quarter	Fourth Quarter
Dues	$3,000	$3,000	$4,500	$6,000
Newsletter	292	292	875	292
Checking interest	40	40	40	40
Conference	0	0	0	7,100
Miscellaneous	0	0	0	0
Total	$3,332	$3,332	$5,415	$13,432

Yearly Totals

Dues	$16,500
Newsletter	1,751
Checking interest	160
Conference	7,100
Miscellaneous	0
Total revenue	$25,511

income was greatest for the newsletter issued before the association's conference in October. On this basis, half of the $1,751 income was budgeted in the third quarter, with the other half distributed evenly over the remaining three quarters. Conference income was received during the fourth quarter, when the conference was held. With an increase in the conference fees for next year, a larger amount of revenue, $7,100, was estimated. Checking interest was distributed evenly across the four quarters. Although some miscellaneous revenue would be received, none was budgeted to reflect the uncertainty of receiving it. Adding together the components of revenue gives a total anticipated revenue of $25,511.

The treasurer then turned attention to association costs. As an example, consider the estimation of costs for publications.

The board's stated goals included programs for publication of a high-quality newsletter to disseminate information of interest to members and publication of a good-quality membership directory. These goals were forwarded to the publications chairperson, who was asked to make recommendations to the board on a proposed budget for each of these publications. In addition, the chairperson was invited to suggest other possible short- and long-term objectives for the association. The publications chairperson was instructed to submit a line-item budget for each publication. The format of the proposed budget was to include specific objectives. For example, the objective was to publish 1,200 newsletters each quarter. Quarterly estimates of costs for each newsletter were to include cost of secretarial expense, printing cost, postage cost, cost of computer-generated labels, and miscellaneous costs. The deadline for submission to the treasurer was set at August 1.

Each officer and each committee chairperson were asked to submit a similar budget proposal for the board's review. The board scheduled a budget meeting for August 15 to prepare the final budget report. Chairpersons of committees were invited to attend. Using the treasurer's estimate of income for the next fiscal year, budgets for each activity were approved, and a line-item budget was prepared.

The final operating budget approved by the board is shown in Exhibit 11-5.

Note that the final amount allocated to the publications committee was $1,000 a quarter for the newsletter, and $1,700 in the third quarter for the annual directory. The

EXHIBIT 11-5

Yearly Budgeted Operating Costs, Year 198X + 1

SHENVALL PROFESSIONAL ASSOCIATION
BUDGET OF OPERATING COSTS, YEAR 198X + 1
JULY 20, 198X

	First Quarter	Second Quarter	Third Quarter	Fourth Quarter
Conferences	$ 600	$ 600	$1,100	$2,400
Administration	865	980	865	865
Publications	1,000	1,000	2,700	1,000
Committees	1,787	1,987	888	888
Computer	300	300	300	300
Miscellaneous	250	250	250	250
Yearly Totals	$4,802	$5,117	$6,103	$5,703

Conferences	$4,700
Administration	3,575
Publications	5,700
Committees	5,550
Computer	1,200
Miscellaneous	1,000
Total costs	$21,725

total budgeted costs for year 198x + 1 is $21,725. With estimated revenue of $25,511, costs of $21,725 provide an estimated surplus of $3,786, or 15 percent of revenues. While this surplus is larger than might be desired in normal years, a budgeted surplus in 198x + 1 larger than past years is realistic in case revenues do not live up to expectations, or to replenish the savings account.

Planning for our budget systematically and using our budget as a cost-control financial statement have served the purposes intended:

1. To evaluate programs in terms of what programs are to be funded

2. To determine realistic costs associated with programs (with a sharp eye on how to cut unnecessary or excessive costs)

3. To provide administrators with decision-making information when problems arise.

APPENDICES

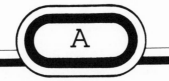

UNDERSTANDING
FINANCIAL STATEMENTS

This appendix is intended for individuals who have little finance and accounting background and for those who desire a review prior to reading the body of the book. Its aim is to overview financial statements, introducing the concepts and vocabulary you will find in the book itself.

Financial statements and financial accounting are oriented toward the stockholders who own the corporation and toward the legal reporting required by the federal government. Financial reporting data are the source of taxation reporting and reporting required by the Securities and Exchange Commission. These data also allow the stockholder and manager to judge how well the overall corporation, and divisions within the corporation, are performing. There are three basic financial accounting reports which your company will include in its annual report. These three reports are: the statement of earnings, the balance sheet, and the statement of changes in financial position. Each will be discussed.

The financial statements that follow are consistent with each other and represent the year-end report of a large company with about $1.3 billion in sales. These statements include all items you are likely to encounter on most companies' financial statements. The financial statements list financial information for a two-year period: the present year and the previous year, so a quick comparison is possible.

As you read the following descriptions of the three basic financial statements, you should refer to the sample statements in Exhibits A–1, A–2, and A–3.

STATEMENT OF EARNINGS

The statement of earnings (often called the profit and loss statement or income statement) identifies the profit and/or loss made by the company in the last time period, such as a year. It is thus a summary of the year's operation. The statement of earnings begins with the revenue to the company and subtracts from it the company costs to leave the profit earned. A sample statement of earnings is shown in Exhibit A–1.

To arrive at net income, the following are subtracted from sales and other income: cost of products sold; selling, research, and administrative expenses; depreciation and amortization; interest expense; and taxes.

Sales and Other Income

Sales is the actual dollars received from customers for the products and services sold. It includes only sales outside the company. Other income is legitimate income to the corporation that must be reported but is not from sales. Other income could include interest income, dividends, or revenue from sale of assets.

EXHIBIT A-1

Sample Earnings Statement

STATEMENT OF EARNINGS

Year ended Dec. 31 (in thousands)	198X	198X − 1
Revenue		
Sales	$1,304,698	$1,395,476
Other income	17,857	19,225
Total revenue	1,322,555	1,414,701
Costs		
Cost of products sold	1,021,808	1,058,640
Selling, research, and administrative expense	123,128	115,188
Depreciation and amortization	76,455	67,662
Interest expense	16,930	18,869
Total costs	1,238,321	1,260,359
Income before taxes	84,234	154,342
Income taxes	27,450	63,630
Net income	56,784	90,712
Dividends:		
Preferred stock [$4.00 per share]	8	8
Common stock [198X—$1.10 per share; 198X − 1—$1.02 per share]	28,360	26,334
Earnings per common share	$2.16	$3.55

Cost of Products Sold

Cost of products sold is all costs associated with manufacturing the products and services sold. These costs include raw material, labor, and overhead. Frequently, products are manufactured for inventory, so the costs of manufacture are charged to inventory. As the products are sold, the costs are transferred to Cost of Products Sold.

Selling, Research, and Administrative Expense

Selling, research, and administrative expense is the costs for these categories, and these costs are grouped so that they can be clearly compared with manufacturing costs. These costs are the total for the company.

Depreciation and Amortization

In theory, depreciation is the decline in the useful value of a capital asset due to wear and tear, obsolescence, and so on. ("Amortization" is used by some companies as an alternate word for "depreciation"; for other companies it is a form of depreciation used for special assets like natural gas wells.) Such depreciation then can be listed as an expense of doing business in the year it occurred. In theory, this lowers profit but makes more cash available to replace the capital asset some time in the future. In practice, most depreciation decisions are made under Internal Revenue Service rules to minimize federal taxes and do not necessarily reflect the actual using up of the capital asset. These costs are included under Depreciation and Amortization.

Interest Expense

Interest expense is interest paid during the fiscal year for company borrowing. It will include current interest paid on long-term debt as well as interest paid on short-term loans necessary to balance cash flow.

Income Taxes

Income taxes are federal (and possibly state and local) income taxes paid on earnings for the fiscal year. The sum of all income taxes paid is included under Income Taxes.

Net Income

Net income is the "bottom line," the profit earned by the company during the fiscal year. Note that for the current year, profit has declined from the previous year, reflecting a decline in sales.

Dividends

Dividends are not really a formal part of the statement of earnings but are often listed here since dividends are the portion of profits paid out in cash to the shareholders. As shown in Exhibit A–1, $8,000 was paid to preferred stockholders (preferred stock is special stock with guaranteed dividends), and $28,360,000 was paid in dividends to common shareholders. The balance of the $56,784,000 profit was retained for future use in the company.

Earnings Per Common Share

Earnings per common share is also not a formal part of the statement of earnings. Many stock investors, however, use the figure along with profits as guides to stock prices. Thus, it is often listed on the statement-of-earnings page. Earnings per common share is calculated by dividing the profit after taxes by the average number of shares of common stock outstanding during the year. The decrease in earnings per common share in Exhibit A–1 from $3.55 in year 198x – 1

EXHIBIT A–2

Sample Balance Sheet

CONSOLIDATED BALANCE SHEET

On December 31 (in thousands)	198X	198X – 1
Assets		
Current assets		
Cash	$ 19,057	$ 9,337
Marketable securities	46,368	88,009
Receivables	124,429	121,938
Inventories	161,923	139,388
Prepaid expenses	10,876	7,101
Total current assets	362,653	365,773
Fixed Assets		
Machinery	993,644	915,727
Buildings	299,129	272,590
Other property, including plant land	61,311	51,628
Total before depreciation	1,354,084	1,239,945
Less accumulated depreciation	609,544	556,439
Total	744,540	683,506
Construction in progress	91,483	79,760
Construction funds held by trustees	1,869	–
Total fixed assets	837,892	763,266
Other assets	8,153	7,318
Total assets	1,208,698	1,136,357
Liabilities and shareholders' equity		
Current liabilities		
Accounts payable and accrued expenses	132,861	109,919
Notes payable and current maturities of long-term obligations	5,984	9,421
Income taxes	11,446	30,973
Total current liabilities	150,291	150,313
Long-term obligations	248,534	244,988
Deferred income taxes	129,539	109,418
Total liabilities	528,364	504,719

Shareholders' equity

Common stock, $5 par, at stated value Shares authorized: 70,000,000		
Shares issued: 24,216,573	212,030	194,125
Retained income	468,733	437,942
Common stock in treasury, at cost		
Shares held: 39,402	[429]	[429]
Total shareholders' equity	680,334	631,638
Total liabilities and shareholders' equity	1,208,698	1,136,357

to $2.16 in year 198x shows the same decline in profit as does the net profit figure.

BALANCE SHEET

The balance sheet represents the financial picture of the company on one particular day, the last day of the fiscal year (December 31, if you are using the calendar year). It is a "snapshot" of the assets and liabilities on that one day, not a summary of the year's activities. The balance sheet is divided into two parts: on the top are shown assets; on the bottom are shown liabilities and stockholders' equity. Both parts must be in balance (equal). In the assets column are listed all goods, properties, and equipment owned as well as claims against others yet to be collected. Under liabilities are listed all debts owed. Under shareholders' equity are listed the liabilities to owners of the corporation, the amount the shareholders would split up if the corporation were liquidated at its balance-sheet value. A sample balance sheet is shown in Exhibit A–2.

Current Assets

Current assets includes the total of those assets that can be converted into cash in a fairly short time period, that is, liquid assets.

Cash.   Cash includes currency and coins on hand and money in checking accounts.

Marketable securities.   Marketable securities represents temporary investment of cash which is not needed immediately. Marketable securities are usually in the form of commercial paper (short-term loans) and government securities and are listed at cost value. The total holdings of the marketable securities of the company are listed under the category Marketable Securities.

Receivables.   Most sales are made on a credit basis, with the customers paying after the products are received. Receivables are the amount of credit sales not paid for at the end of the fiscal year. Receivables will be adjusted slightly to allow for bad debts. The total of accounts receivable held by the company is listed under Receivables.

Inventories.   Inventory is composed of four components: raw materials to be used in products, partially finished goods in process of manufacture, finished goods awaiting shipment to customers, and disposable items and spare parts to be used in manufacturing. Inventories are listed at cost value. The total of all inventories held by the company is listed under Inventories.

Prepaid expenses.   Prepaid expenses includes all items paid in advance of receipt of goods and services. They are items that will be charged as expenses in the next fiscal year.

Fixed Assets

Fixed assets includes those assets that cannot be readily converted into cash.

Machinery, buildings, and other property. These categories include owned assets recorded at cost and the cost value of leased assets.

Accumulated depreciation. Accumulated depreciation is the depreciation accumulated from current and past income statements. It represents the total amount of the assets written off as expenses to date.

Construction in progress. Construction in progress is listed as a separate asset category to identify it clearly and to recognize that these assets are not yet available to earn income.

Construction funds held by trustees. This category includes funds currently held by a third party (trustee) that will eventually be paid to a firm doing construction work for the company.

Other Assets

Other assets includes owned items that do not fall neatly into other categories. An example might be minority investments in other firms. Intangible assets, like goodwill, are not listed since their value cannot be determined or justified.

Total Assets

Total assets includes the sum of all the current, fixed, and other assets to provide a picture of the total investment in the company.

LIABILITIES

Current Liabilities

Current liabilities includes those debts that are due in a short time, generally the next year.

Accounts payable. Accounts payable represents those items purchased on credit and not paid on the day the balance sheet was calculated, December 31. This item is necessary when a firm uses the accrual accounting system and buys many of its raw materials and supplies on credit.

Notes payable. Notes payable includes short-term loans, bonds, and so on, that must be repaid in the next year. This category also includes that portion of long-term debt that will become due in the next fiscal year.

Income taxes. This item includes income taxes owed but not paid by the end of the fiscal year. These taxes will be paid in the next fiscal year.

Long-Term Obligations

Long-term obligations includes bonds, loans, and other obligations that are due in years beyond the next fiscal year. They are a legitimate debt of the corporation, but a debt not due in the immediate future.

Deferred Income Taxes

Deferred income taxes includes those taxes that are already owed but need not be paid until after the next fiscal year.

Under the accrual accounting system, taxes are considered owed during the fiscal year when the profit is earned. Under tax laws, however, some taxes, particularly investment and energy tax credits, are deferred; that is, they are not due until some time in the future.

SHAREHOLDERS' EQUITY

Common Stock

Common stock identifies the investment the original owners have made in the corporation. Note that more shares of stock have been authorized than have been issued. Thus, the corporation could issue more shares and sell them to increase cash, if needed. Such shares would be sold at the current market price, not at the par value of $5. Selling too much authorized stock would drive down the value of the current outstanding shares.

The stockholders have also authorized the issuance of preferred stock, but only a small amount is outstanding. It is included in the long-term obligations above.

Retained Income

Retained income is the sum of all the profits over the history of the company that have been reinvested in the company. It is the sum of all profits that have not been paid out as dividends.

Retained income is a form of owners' equity and hence a liability. It may already have been used for investment in the past. That portion of retained income currently available for use is included under cash and marketable securities on the assets side of the balance sheet.

Treasury Stock

The value of treasury stock held by the corporation is listed here at cost. When a corporation holds some of its own stock, the stock is really an asset of the firm. Rather than list it as an asset, however, accounting theory treats it as a negative liability. Thus, on the balance sheet, treasury stock is listed as negative shareholders' equity.

Total Liabilities and Shareholders' Equity

Total liabilities and shareholders' equity includes the sum of all the money the company owes, either to creditors or to owners. This figure must be equal to the total assets for the balance sheet to be correct.

STATEMENT OF CHANGES IN FINANCIAL POSITION

The statement of changes in financial position is most often made up of two sub-statements: (1) the funds flow or cash flow statement, and (2) the changes-in-working-capital statement. The statement of changes in financial position is less standardized among companies than the earnings statement and the balance sheet. A representative statement including the elements used in most companies is shown in Exhibit A–3.

In Exhibit A–3, two major statements are provided: (1) the sources and use of funds and (2) an analysis of changes in working capital.

Sources and Uses of Funds

The sources-and-uses-of-funds statement summarizes the inflow and outflow of funds over the fiscal year.

EXHIBIT A–3

Sample Changes in Financial Position

STATEMENT OF CHANGES IN FINANCIAL POSITION

Year ended Dec. 31 (in thousands)

	198X	198X − 1
Sources of funds:		
Net income	$56,784	$90,712
Provision for depreciation and amortization	76,455	67,662
Provision for deferred income taxes	22,495	15,602
Funds generated from operations	155,734	173,976
Common stock issued	17,905	9,896
Increase in long-term obligations	17,140	8,529
Value of assets sold	2,622	2,801
Other transactions	[834]	1,682
Total sources of funds	192,567	196,884
Uses of funds:		
Additions to plant	151,835	133,115
Dividends	28,360	26,334
Construction funds deposited with trustees	7,906	—
Reduction in long-term obligations	7,566	9,278
Total uses of funds	195,667	168,727
Increase [decrease] in funds	[3,100]	28,157
Analysis of changes in working capital:		
Increase [decrease] in current assets:		
Cash and marketable securities	[31,921]	20,426
Receivables	2,490	9,276
Inventories	22,534	19,478
Prepaid expenses	3,775	[11,362]
Total changes	[3,122]	[37,818]

[Increase] decrease in current liabilities:		
Accounts payable and accrued expenses	[22,942]	[12,028]
Notes payable and current maturities of long-term obligations	3,437	[3,022]
Income taxes	19,527	5,389
Total changes	22	[9,661]
Increase [decrease] in working capital	[3,100]	28,157
Working capital:		
At beginning of year	215,461	187,304
At end of year	212,361	215,461

Funds generated from operations. Funds generated from operations include funds which are generated in cash from the current year's activities. These funds include: (1) net income (profit after taxes), (2) depreciation (depreciation is an expense of doing business, but the cash is not actually paid to anyone), and (3) deferred taxes.

Other sources of funds. Sources of funds other than funds from operations, are also listed. Common stock sold brings cash for the company to use, as does more long-term borrowing. Sales of assets are also a source of funds.

Finally, other miscellaneous transactions could include cash from sale of minority interests in other companies, or a profit made on foreign currency transactions. If such transactions resulted in a financial loss, a negative figure would be reported. An example would be foreign currency sold at a loss rather than at a profit.

Adding the sources of funds together gives a total source of funds.

Uses of Funds

The cash brought into the company can be used for a number of purposes. One is for additions to plant, facilities, and equipment. A second is for dividends. Construction funds deposited with trustees also tie up funds. Finally, cash may be used to repay long-term debt, resulting in a reduction of long-term debt.

Adding together these uses of funds results in a total amount of funds used.

Increase [Decrease] in Funds

Subtracting the funds used from the funds gained gives the increase or decrease in funds. In the example in Exhibit A–3, funds decreased by $3,100,000 during the year. Since total funds were about $212,000,000, this is a small decrease. This means that the company paid out more money than it took in. This is possible because the company had enough cash on hand on the first of the year to cover this small decrease.

Changes in Working Capital

The changes-in-working-capital statement calculates the changes in current assets and current liabilities from the end of the previous fiscal year to the end of the current fiscal year. The analysis of working capital shown in Exhibit A–3 is an additional way of expressing the same cash flow data as in the sources-and-uses-of-funds statement, so the overall result must be the same.

Increase [Decrease] in current assets. From the end of one fiscal year to the end of the next, cash and marketable securities dropped by $31,921,000, while accounts receivable, inventories, and prepaid expenses all increased, resulting in a net decrease in current assets of $3,122,000. Note that most of the increase was in inventories, suggesting an overall decrease in cash to build up inventories.

[Increase] Decrease in current liabilities.
Over the last fiscal year, accounts payable increased by approximately $23 million, while notes payable and income taxes decreased by about the same amount, resulting in a net decrease in current liabilities of $22,000.

Increase [Decrease] in Working Capital

Subtracting the decrease in total liabilities from the decrease in total assets gives a total decrease in working capital of $3,100,000. Note that this is the same as the decrease in funds also shown in Exhibit A–3. This is a small amount compared to the total funds flow.

Working Capital

Although really not a part of either statement, a summary of working capital is usually added to give a feel for the magnitude of the money involved. Thus, approximately $212 million is available at the start of the new fiscal year in working capital.

FINANCIAL STATEMENTS REVISITED

Financial statements are intended to give an overview of the financial health of the company. You do not need to understand them perfectly, but an understanding of them will aid your ability to use the budgeting process detailed in this book.

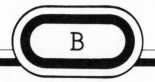

BUDGETING BY
COMPUTERS
AND SPREADSHEETS

INTRODUCTION

Planning, developing, and revising a budget are critical to companies and managers. It is thus not surprising that the increased use of computers over the last ten years has included, as an application, the use of the computer to perform many budgeting functions. We discussed budgeting in the body of this book, emphasizing the concepts and the techniques to develop the details. We did all the work by hand, to emphasize that the mechanics of developing and revising a budget do not require complex arithmetic and that budget calculations are well within the skills of all supervisors and managers.

By the middle 1970s, most large organizations had switched their budgeting formats and data gathering techniques to computers. A typical system would require managers and supervisors to provide their input to the accounting department on handwritten sheets. The data would be entered on the computer by the accounting or data processing department. Other data inputs, such as from time sheets, material requisitions, and purchase orders, would also be entered into the computer. The computer would then print the monthly budgets and the variance-analysis reports. If the budget needed to be revised, the department supervisor would perform the calculations by hand and return the new hand calculations to the accounting department for data entry. This system (central-accounting computer budget and department supervisor manual revision) is still probably the most widely used budgeting and budget revision system.

By the mid 1980s, both large company computers and the increased availability of microcomputers offered aids to managers in budgeting.

COMPANY COMPUTERS

The budgeting programs available on company mainframe computers are normally part of a complete financial accounting and management program. The production data entered for a department budget also become part of the profit-and-loss estimate, the funds flow statement, and the inventory control estimates. In most of the systems, however, the operating supervisor or manager still does not have direct access to the computer program and must provide new and revised data to the computer through the accounting department.

In a few companies now (and many more in the near future), operating supervisors or managers are (or will be) given a computer terminal for their offices. This computer terminal allows direct access to the company budgeting program, as well as to many other programs. At the direction of the accounting department, when changes are necessary, the supervisors can call up their budgets and update or change the budgets right on the terminal. In many cases, for variable cost data, the supervisor could simply enter the change in production quantity, and the computer could calculate the new dollar amount. Caution! Use of one budgeting program for the entire company means the program may include many items not needed in any one specific department or cost center.

The computer programs companies use are often written specifically for the company and vary greatly. It would be of little use to look at a specific computer program example here. The example that will be shown for microcomputers in this appendix, however, shows the approach that most programs for larger computers would follow.

SPREADSHEETS

To develop a budget by hand, most people would buy special accounting paper with rows and columns already printed on it. They would then put headings on the rows and columns and fill in the numerical data in the center of the form. The spreadsheets developed for microcomputers are basically the equivalent of the printed accounting paper. The user calls onto the screen a blank form with rows and columns marked, puts headings on the rows and columns, and fills in the numerical data in the center. One feature of most spreadsheet programs is that the program can be written to perform some of the arithmetic calculations for you.

There are many spreadsheet programs on the market today, ranging in price from $95 to $895. The more expensive programs usually have a great deal more flexibility. Caution! Spreadsheet programs tend to be written for a specific model of a specific microcomputer. You need to make sure you buy a spreadsheet that will work on the computer you have.

You can purchase a microcomputer in two basic ways. You can buy one with your own money and use it at home. You can also buy a microcomputer with company money and use it for a number of applications in your office.

You can also develop the details of your spreadsheet in

two basic ways. You can develop it as a duplicate of the company budget format, and develop and revise your department budget on it, giving the printed output to the accounting department for entry on the company mainframe computer. You can also develop a spreadsheet different from the company format, use it to make the calculations you desire, and then mark up by hand an old company budget form to give to the accounting department.

You should *not* expect to be able to connect your microcomputer to the company computer. In general, these connections are difficult unless a great deal of planning goes into making sure the computers are compatible. A good rule of thumb is that most combinations of computers are not compatible unless deliberately designed to be so.

If you are budgeting for a smaller company or organization, you may find a microcomputer is adequate for all your accounting purposes. In this case, a purchased microcomputer spreadsheet program may allow the entire organization to handle its budget using the same program.

Regardless of how you might handle your budget by computer, an example of budget development and revision by spreadsheet will provide insight to computer budgeting on both large and small computers. The example below includes elements common to all spreadsheet programs (they tend to be very similar), but is not modeled after any one program.

In Chapter 6, we developed a budget for a new department of our Harrisonburg Office Equipment Manufacturing Company, the computer-tables department. In Chapter 8, we revised this budget. In both cases, we performed all the calculations by hand to emphasize the concepts to follow and to emphasize the details in calculation of the data. Once you are familiar with the calculation techniques, there is no great need for you to repeat them each time you develop a new month's budget or revise an existing budget. Use of a computer model allows you to minimize your work.

In this section, we will develop October's budget for the computer-tables department in the way you would develop it using the spreadsheet concept. We assume you have read the body of this book; if you have not, much we say will have little meaning. A review of Chapters 6 and 8 would increase what you will learn from this appendix.

The budget for the computer-tables department for October, as developed in Chapter 6, is repeated in Exhibit B–1. This figure must be the same as the final computer-developed output.

SPREADSHEET DEVELOPMENT PROCEDURE

The procedure to develop a spreadsheet budget can be broken down into five steps. The first is to develop the form of the budget printout and the row and column headings. The second step is to determine the fixed content fields. (The types of content fields will be defined shortly.) Next is to determine the variable estimated content fields, followed by determining the variable calculated content fields. The fifth and final step is to execute the program to calculate all values and print (or display) the output.

1. Budget Form and Row and Column Headings

The first step in designing your spreadsheet budget is to develop the form of the budget printout you wish. This generally means making a draft by hand to identify the chosen form and then entering it into the computer using a specific, already written computer (spreadsheet) program. We will not discuss the details of any specific computer program, but will present an approach common to almost all spreadsheets.

EXHIBIT B-1

Sample Department Budget, October

HARRISONBURG OFFICE EQUIP. MANU. CO.
COST-CENTER BUDGET
COST CENTER 22, COMPUTER-TABLES DEPARTMENT
OCTOBER, 198X

Item		Unit	Quantity	Cost	Total
1.1	Hourly labor	hours	3,432	$7.63	$26,170
1.2	Salaried labor				2,000
1.3	Overtime	hours			0
1.4	Benefits				10,346
1.5	Repair labor	hours	140	9.93	1,390
2.1	Repair materials				200
3.1	Miscellaneous				1,000
4.1	Process supplies				5,310
5.1	Outside services				0
6.1	Utilities				810
7.1	Depreciation				6,667
8.1	Production materials:				
8.11	Wood				11,789
8.12	Metal				9,087
8.13	Other				2,462
9.1	Factory indirect-cost allocation				12,012
10.1	Total				$89,243

Production:	T-11 units	400
	T-12 units	400
	T-13 units	400
	T-14 units	400

The main task in designing the budget form is to assign headings to the rows and columns you wish in the output report. Every row and column must have a heading. We will assume for this example that each heading must be exactly four characters long and must start with an alphabetic character. (Assumptions like these are required for all spreadsheet programs.) Exhibit B–2 shows a heading assignment for each row and column superimposed on the budget form developed in Chapter 6 and shown in Exhibit B–1.

The budget form is broken into two parts. The headings at the top (company title, budget heading, department identification, and month) are given row headings of "COMP," "CCBU," "CCNO," and "DATE," respectively, but are all under one column heading, "FORM." The body of the report form has twenty-two row headings and five column headings. As you can see, the headings were picked to be like the actual titles in English. Thus "HRLA" is the row heading in which "ITEM" (1.1 Hourly Labor), "UNIT" (hrs), "QUAN" (Quantity), "UTCO" (Cost), and "TOTL" (Total) are the column headings. Each piece of data to be entered on the budget form must be identified by a row and column location. Thus, the total hourly-labor dollar amount would be listed in the program as the intersection of the symbols "HRLA, TOTL."

In developing an original budget from the beginning, you would not have the already developed manual budget to start with. A more realistic starting point than Exhibit B–2 might be that shown in Exhibit B–3.

In Exhibit B–3, the row and column headings are listed as in Exhibit B–2. In the center of the table (often called the "matrix" of the table) you set up the types of data that will go into the table. Three types of data are shown here. "Fixx" (again, the abbreviations must be exactly four characters) indicates a fixed content field; that is, a field with data that will not change each time the program is executed. "Vest" indicates a variable content field that you must es-

EXHIBIT B-2

Spreadsheet Format Titles on Department Budget Form

FORM
COMP   HARRISONBURG OFFICE EQUIP. MANU. CO.
CCBU   COST-CENTER BUDGET
CCNO COST CENTER 22, COMPUTER-TABLES DEPARTMENT
DATE   OCTOBER, 198X

TITL	ITEM Item		UNIT Unit	QUAN Quantity	UTCO Cost	TOTL Total
HRLA	1.1	Hourly labor	hours	3,432	$7.63	$26,170
SALA	1.2	Salaried labor				2,000
OVER	1.3	Overtime	hours			0
BENE	1.4	Benefits				10,346
RELA	1.5	Repair labor	hours	140	9.93	1,390
REMT	2.1	Repair materials				200
MISC	3.1	Miscellaneous				1,000
PRSU	4.1	Process supplies				5,310
OUSE	5.1	Outside services				0
UTIL	6.1	Utilities				810
DEPR	7.1	Depreciation				6,667
PRMT	8.1	Production materials:				
WOOD	8.11	Wood				11,789
METL	8.12	Metal				9,087
OTHR	8.13	Other				2,462
FAIN	9.1	Factory indirect-cost allocation				12,012
TOTA	10.1	Total				$89,243
T-11		Production:	T-11 units	400		
T-12			T-12 units	400		
T-13			T-13 units	400		
T-14			T-14 units	400		

timate each time you develop or revise a budget. "Vcal" indicates a variable calculated content field. If you program the computer with appropriate equations, the computer will calculate these values and fill in their locations in the matrix for you.

You must review each row and column intersection and determine what kind of data type, if any, goes into that location. A row and column intersection is often called a "cell" of the matrix. Thus, the row and column cell of "UTIL,ITEM" is a fixed content field ("Fixx") because the data entry in that cell, "6.1 Utilities," will not change each time the program is executed. On the other hand, the cell "SALA,TOTL" is the salaried labor cost you must estimate each month, and hence is a variable estimated content field ("Vest"). Finally, the cell "TOTA,TOTL" is the total monthly budget calculated by adding up all the budget lines. The computer can calculate this value once all the budget lines are filled in, so this cell is a variable calculated content field ("Vcal").

2. Spreadsheet Fixed Content Fields

Once you have determined the fixed content fields you desire, you can enter the data for each fixed content cell on the terminal screen. The computer will remember what you desire in each location and keep it there and print it out each time until you deliberately change it. Exhibit B–4 shows the data you would enter in each fixed content field for our example.

For example, in location "COMP,FORM" we would like the company name, the Harrisonburg Office Equip Man. Co. In location "UTIL,ITEM" we would like the row title of "6.1 Utilities" to be printed.

Exhibit B–5 shows what our budget form would look like at this stage with the row and column headings printed and with all the fixed content fields from Exhibit B–4 filled in.

EXHIBIT B-3

Spreadsheet Format, Content Field Identification

		FORM
COMP		Fixx
CCBU		Fixx
CCNO		Fixx
DATE		Vest

	ITEM	UNIT	QUAN	UTCO	TOTL
TITL	Fixx	Fixx	Fixx	Fixx	Fixx
HRLA	Fixx	Fixx	Vcal	Vcal	Vcal
SALA	Fixx				Vest
OVER	Fixx	Fixx	Vest	Vest	Vcal
BENE	Fixx				Vcal
RELA	Fixx	Fixx	Vest	Vest	Vcal
REMT	Fixx				Vest
MISC	Fixx				Vest
PRSU	Fixx				Vest
OUSE	Fixx				Vest
UTIL	Fixx				Vest
DEPR	Fixx				Vest
PRMT	Fixx				
WOOD	Fixx				Vcal
METL	Fixx				Vcal
OTHR	Fixx				Vcal
FAIN	Fixx				Vcal
TOTA	Fixx				Vcal
T-11	Fixx		Vest		
T-12	Fixx		Vest		
T-13	Fixx		Vest		
T-14	Fixx		Vest		

EXHIBIT B–4

Spreadsheet Fixed Content Fields

FIXED CONTENT FIELDS (Fixx)

Form Headings:

COMP, FORM = HARRISONBURG OFFICE EQUIP.
MANU. CO.
CCBU, FORM = COST-CENTER BUDGET
CCNO, FORM = COST CENTER 22, COMPUTER-
TABLES DEPARTMENT

Column Headings:

TITL, ITEM = Item
TITL, UNIT = Unit
TITL, QUAN = Quantity
TITL, UTCO = Cost
TITL, TOTL = Total

Row Headings:

HRLA, ITEM = 1.1 Hourly labor
SALA, ITEM = 1.2 Salaried labor
OVER, ITEM = 1.3 Overtime
BENE, ITEM = 1.4 Benefits
RELA, ITEM = 1.5 Repair labor
REMT, ITEM = 2.1 Repair materials
MISC, ITEM = 3.1 Miscellaneous
PRSU, ITEM = 4.1 Process supplies
OUSE, ITEM = 5.1 Outside services
UTIL, ITEM = 6.1 Utilities
DEPR, ITEM = 7.1 Depreciation
PRMT, ITEM = 8.1 Production materials
WOOD, ITEM = 8.11 Wood
METL, ITEM = 8.12 Metal
OTHR, ITEM = 8.13 Other
FAIN, ITEM = 9.1 Factory indirect-cost allocation
TOTA, ITEM = 10.1 Total
T–11, ITEM = Production: T–11 units

T–12, ITEM	=	T–12 units
T–13, ITEM	=	T–13 units
T–14, ITEM	=	T–14 units

Items in Body of Matrix:

HRLA, UNIT	=	hours
OVER, UNIT	=	hours
RELA, UNIT	=	hours

Notice that Exhibit B–5 shows the cells for "Vest" and "Vcal" still to be filled in.

3. Spreadsheet Variable Estimated Content Fields

The next step in developing our budget would be to estimate the data we must estimate each time the budget is developed or revised. These estimates are shown in Exhibit B–6.

As an example, in Exhibit B–6 we see that "T-11,QUAN" is one of the estimates we must fill in. "T-11,QUAN" is the planned production of computer table T-11 for October. Also listed in Exhibit B–6 are the actual dollar estimates for October already discussed in Chapter 6. Thus, for "T-11,QUAN" we are planning 400 units of production in October.

You must fill in each of these estimates the first time you develop the budget. For future months' budgets and for budget revisions, you can start by calling up the old budget and changing only the estimates that need to be changed.

Exhibit B–7 shows the budget form with the estimates of Exhibit B–6 added. Note that the "Vcal" cells still remain to be filled.

EXHIBIT B-5

Spreadsheet With Fixed Content Fields Listed

```
                         FORM
COMP        HARRISONBURG OFFICE EQUIP. MANU. CO.
CCBU                COST-CENTER BUDGET
CCNO COST CENTER 22, COMPUTER-TABLES DEPARTMENT
DATE                    OCTOBER, 198X
```

TITL	ITEM Item		UNIT Unit	QUAN Quantity	UTCO Cost	TOTL Total
HRLA	1.1	Hourly labor	hours	Vcal	Vcal	Vcal
SALA	1.2	Salaried labor				Vest
OVER	1.3	Overtime	hours	Vest	Vest	Vcal
BENE	1.4	Benefits				Vcal
RELA	1.5	Repair labor	hours	Vest	Vest	Vcal
REMT	2.1	Repair materials				Vest
MISC	3.1	Miscellaneous				Vest
PRSU	4.1	Process supplies				Vest
OUSE	5.1	Outside services				Vest
UTIL	6.1	Utilities				Vest
DEPR	7.1	Depreciation				Vest
PRMT	8.1	Production materials:				
WOOD	8.11	Wood				Vcal
METL	8.12	Metal				Vcal
OTHR	8.13	Other				Vcal
FAIN	9.1	Factory indirect-cost allocation				Vcal
TOTA	10.1	Total				Vcal
T-11		Production: T-11 units		Vest		
T-12		T-12 units		Vest		
T-13		T-13 units		Vest		
T-14		T-14 units		Vest		

EXHIBIT B–6

Spreadsheet Variable Estimated Content Fields (Vest)

In headings:
    DATE, FORM = ?   (for October, OCTOBER, 198X)

Production:
        T–11, QUAN = ?   (for October, 400)
        T–12, QUAN = ?   (for October, 400)
        T–13, QUAN = ?   (for October, 400)
        T–14, QUAN = ?   (for October, 400)

In body of matrix:
        SALA, TOTL = ?   (for October, $2,000)
        OVER, QUAN = ?   (for October, 0 hrs)
        OVER, UTCO = ?   (for October, 0)
        RELA, QUAN = ?   (for October, 140 hrs)
        RELA, UTCO = ?   (for October, $9.93)
        REMT, TOTL = ?   (for October, $200)
        MISC, TOTL = ?   (for October, $1,000)
        PRSU, TOTL = ?   (for October, $5,310)
        OUSE, TOTL = ?   (for October, 0)
        UTIL, TOTL = ?   (for October, $810)
        DEPR, TOTL = ?   (for October, $6,667)

4. Spreadsheet Variable
Calculated Content Fields

All of the "Vcal" cells are data that the computer can calculate for you, if you give the computer the formulas to
calculate the data. All of the data for the calculations must
already be part of the form ("Fixx" or "Vest") or included
in the calculation formula. Exhibit B–8 shows the formulas
for all the "Vcal" cells shown in earlier figures.

All of the formulas are derived from information presented or calculated in Chapters 6 and 8. (Numbers may vary slightly due to rounding error.) In addition, the exact data for October are calculated for each formula. For example, "HRLA,QUAN," the number of hourly labor hours required to produce all products is equal to (2.2 hrs) (T-11,QUAN) + (2.2 hrs) (T-12,QUAN) + (2.31 hrs) (T-13,QUAN) + (1.87 hrs) (T-14,QUAN). That is, for each product the labor hours required to produce that product is multiplied by the number of units to be produced. (For product T-11, this is (2.2) (T-11,QUAN). The sum of the four products are then added to give the total hourly labor hours, "HRLA,QUAN." As shown in Exhibit B–8, these calculations show 3,432 hourly labor hours should be budgeted for October.

As another example, the factory indirect-cost allocation is allocated to each department at the rate of $3.50 per hourly labor hour. In formula notation, "FAIN,TOTL" = ($3.50) (HRLA,QUAN). Thus for October, "FAIN,TOTL" equals (3.5) (3,432), or $12,012.

5. Executing the Spreadsheet Program

After all the fixed content fields, variable estimated content fields, and formulas for calculation are entered, you give the computer a command to execute (carry out) the program. The program calculates all the variable calculated content fields and prints the entire budget report. The finished report with the cells filled in showing the results of Exhibit B–8's calculations is the same as that shown in Exhibit B–2. Most people prefer the budget report without the computer row and title headings. These row and title headings can be suppressed to give the report shown in Exhibit B–1.

Note again! The budget report in Exhibit B–1 must be the same whether it is calculated manually or by computer.

EXHIBIT B-7

Spreadsheet with Fixed and Estimated Content Fields

FORM
COMP HARRISONBURG OFFICE EQUIP. MANU. CO.
CCBU COST-CENTER BUDGET
CCNO COST CENTER 22, COMPUTER-TABLES DEPARTMENT
DATE OCTOBER, 198X

TITL	ITEM Item		UNIT Unit	QUAN Quantity	UTCO Cost	TOTL Total
HRLA	1.1	Hourly labor	hours	Vcal	Vcal	Vcal
SALA	1.2	Salaried labor				$2,000
OVER	1.3	Overtime	hours	0	0	Vcal
BENE	1.4	Benefits				Vcal
RELA	1.5	Repair labor	hours	140	9.93	Vcal
REMT	2.1	Repair materials				200
MISC	3.1	Miscellaneous				1,000
PRSU	4.1	Process supplies				5,310
OUSE	5.1	Outside services				0
UTIL	6.1	Utilities				810
DEPR	7.1	Depreciation				6,667
PRMT	8.1	Production materials:				
WOOD	8.11	Wood				Vcal
METL	8.12	Metal				Vcal
OTHR	8.13	Other				Vcal
FAIN	9.1	Factory indirect-cost allocation				Vcal
TOTA	10.1	Total				Vcal

T-11	Production: T-11 units	400
T-12	T-12 units	400
T-13	T-13 units	400
T-14	T-14 units	400

EXHIBIT B-8

Spreadsheet Variable Calculated Content Fields (Vcal)

In body of matrix:

HRLA, QUAN
= (2.2 hrs) (T–11, QUAN) + (2.2 hrs) (T–12, QUAN) + (2.31 hrs) (T–13, QUAN) + (1.87 hrs) (T–14, QUAN)
= (2.2) (400) + (2.2) (400) + (2.31) (400) + (1.87) (400) = 3,432 hrs (for October)

HRLA, UTCO
= (HRLA, TOTL) / (HRLA, QUAN)
= $26,170 / 3,432 hrs = $7.63/hr (for October)

HRLA, TOTL
= ($16.92) (T–11, QUAN) + ($16.43) (T–12, QUAN) + ($17.93) (T–13, QUAN) + ($14.15) (T–14, QUAN)
= (16.92) (400) + (16.43) (400) + (17.93) (400) + (14.15) (400) = $26,170 (for October)

OVER, TOTL
= (OVER, QUAN) (OVER, UTCO)
= (0) (0) = 0 (for October)

BENE, TOTL
= ($.35) (HRLA, TOTL + SALA, TOTL + RELA, TOTL)
= (.35) (26,170 + 2,000 + 1,390) = $10,346 (for October)

RELA, TOTL
= (RELA, QUAN) (REAL, UTCO)
= (140) (9.93) = $1,390 (for October)

WOOD, TOTL
= ($17.01) (T–12, QUAN) + ($12.42) (T–14, QUAN)
= ($17.01) (400) + (12.42) (400) = $11,789 (for October)

METL, TOTL
= ($13.17) (T–11, QUAN) + ($9.51) (T–13, QUAN)
= (13.17) (400) + (9.51) (400) = $9,087 (for October)

OTHR, TOTL = ($.82) (T–11, QUAN + T–13, QUAN) + ($1.02) (T–12, QUAN + T–14, QUAN) + ($1.24) (T–13, QUAN + T–14, QUAN)
= (.82) (400 + 400) + (1.02) (400 + 400) + (1.24) (400 + 400) = $2,462 (for October)

FAIN, TOTL = ($3.50) (HRLA, QUAN)
= (3.50) (3,432) = $12,012 (for October)

TOTA, TOTL = HRLA, TOTL + SALA, TOTL + OVER, TOTL + BENE, TOTL + RELA, TOTL + REMT, TOTL + MISC, TOTL + PRSU, TOTL + OUSE, TOTL + UTIL, TOTL + DEPR, TOTAL + WOOD, TOTL + METL, TOTL + OTHR, TOTL + FAIN, TOTL
= 26,170 + 2,000 + 0 + 10,346 + 1,390 + 200 + 1,000 + 5,310 + 0 + 810 + 6,667 + 11,789 + 9,087 + 2,462 + 12,012 = $89,243 (for October)

BUDGET PLANNING AND REVISIONS

One of the biggest advantages of setting up the budget by computer is the amount of time and work that can be saved in updating and revising budgets. Once you have the budget program working, you need only change any estimates you desire and have the computer calculate the remaining data. For example, you can experiment with different production levels to determine how they will affect your costs. You can also revise future budgets quickly based upon variance-analysis reports and changing conditions.

CAUTION ON THE
USE OF SPREADSHEETS

Spreadsheet-type programs on both company mainframe computers and microcomputers are very useful tools. They are just that, however—tools to carry out the concepts you already understand. If the concepts are not clear in your mind, use of computer models will only hinder your improving your budgeting process.

BIBLIOGRAPHY

For further study on any of the topics discussed in this book, consult these books.

Gambino, Anthony J., and Thomas J. Reardon. *Financial Planning and Evaluation for the Nonprofit Organization*. New York: American Association of Accountants, 1981.

Herbst, Anthony F. *Capital Budgeting*. New York: Harper & Row, 1982.

Matthews, Lawrence M. *Practical Operating Budgeting*. New York: McGraw-Hill, 1977.

Sweeny, H. W., Allen and Robert Rachling. *Handbook of Budgeting*. New York: John Wiley & Sons, 1981.

Welsch, Glenn A. *Budgeting*. Englewood Cliffs, NJ: Prentice-Hall, 1971.

INDEX

SKILLS FOR SUCCESS